THE GOD
YOU MAY
NOT
KNOW

D1247886

DR. DAVID JEREMIAH

with Dr. David Jeremiah

CONTENTS

ABOUT
DR. DAVID JEREMIAH
AND TURNING POINT

D
r. David Jeremiah is the founder of Turning Point, a ministry committed to providing Christians with sound Bible teaching relevant to today's changing times through radio and television broadcasts, audio series, books, and live events. Dr. Jeremiah's common-sense teaching on topics such as family, prayer, worship, angels, and biblical prophecy forms the foundation of Turning Point.

David and his wife, Donna, reside in El Cajon, California, where he serves as the senior pastor of Shadow Mountain Community Church. David and Donna have four children and twelve grandchildren.

In 1982, Dr. Jeremiah brought the same solid teaching to San Diego television that he shares weekly with his congregation. Shortly thereafter, Turning Point expanded its ministry to radio. Dr. Jeremiah's inspiring messages can now be heard worldwide on radio, television, and the Internet.

Because Dr. Jeremiah desires to know his listening audience, he travels nationwide holding ministry events that touch the hearts and lives of many people. According to Dr. Jeremiah, "At some point in time, everyone reaches a turning point; and for every person, that moment is unique, an experience to hold onto forever. There's so much changing in today's world that sometimes it's difficult to choose the right path. Turning Point offers people an understanding of God's Word as well as the opportunity to make a difference in their lives."

Dr. Jeremiah has authored numerous books, including *Escape the Coming Night* (Revelation), *The Handwriting on the Wall* (Daniel), *Overcoming Loneliness, God in You* (Holy Spirit), *When Your World Falls Apart, 31 Days to Happiness—Searching for Heaven on Earth, Captured by Grace, What in the World Is Going On?, The Coming Economic Armageddon, I Never Thought I'd See the Day!, Agents of the Apocalypse, RESET—Ten Steps to Spiritual Renewal, Ten Questions Christians Are Asking, People Are Asking...Is This the End?* and *A Life Beyond Amazing.*

How to Use This Study Guide

The purpose of this Turning Point study guide is to reinforce Dr. David Jeremiah's dynamic, in-depth teaching and to aid the reader in applying biblical truth to his or her daily life. This study guide is designed to be used in conjunction with Dr. Jeremiah's *The God You May Not Know* audio series, but it may also be used by itself for personal or group study.

Structure of the Lessons

Each lesson is based on one of the messages in the *The God You May Not Know* compact disc series and focuses on specific passages in the Bible. Each lesson is composed of the following elements:

- *Outline*

The outline at the beginning of the lesson gives a clear, concise picture of the topic being studied and provides a helpful framework for readers as they listen to Dr. Jeremiah's teaching.

- *Overview*

The overview summarizes Dr. Jeremiah's teaching on the passage being studied in the lesson. Readers should refer to the Scripture passages in their own Bibles as they study the overview. Unless otherwise indicated, Scripture verses quoted are taken from the New King James Version.

- *Personal and Group Application Questions*

This section contains a variety of questions designed to help readers dig deeper into the lesson and the Scriptures and to apply the lesson to their daily lives. For Bible study groups or Sunday school classes, these questions will provide a springboard for group discussion and interaction.

- *Did You Know?*

This section presents a fascinating fact, historical note, or insight that adds a point of interest to the preceding lesson.

Personal Study

Thank you for selecting *The God You May Not Know* for your current study. The lessons in this study guide were created to help you gain fresh insights into God's Word and develop new perspectives on topics you may have previously studied. Each lesson is designed to challenge your thinking, and help you grow in your knowledge of Christ. During your study, it is our prayer that you will discover how biblical truth affects every aspect of your life and your relationship with Christ will be strengthened.

When you commit to completing this study guide, try to set apart a time, daily or weekly, to read through the lessons without distraction. Have your Bible nearby when you read the study guide, so you're ready to look up verses if you need to. If you want to use a notebook to write down your thoughts, be sure to have that handy as well. Take your time to think through and answer the questions. If you plan on reading the study guide with a small group, be sure to read ahead and be prepared to take part in the weekly discussions.

Leader's Guide

Thank you for your commitment to lead a group through *The God You May Not Know*. Being a leader has its own rewards. You may discover that your walk with the Lord deepens through this experience. Throughout the study guide, your group will explore new topics and review study questions that encourage thought-provoking group discussion.

The lessons in this study guide are suitable for Sunday school classes, small-group studies, elective Bible studies, or home Bible study groups. Each lesson is structured to provoke thought and help you grow in your knowledge and understanding of God. There are multiple components in this section that can help you structure your lessons and discussion time, so make sure you read and consider each one.

Before You Begin

Before you begin each meeting, make sure you and your group are well-versed with the content of the chapter. Every person should have his or her own study guide so they can follow along and write in the study guide if need be. When possible, the study guide should be used with the corresponding compact disc series. You may wish to assign the study guide lesson as homework prior to the meeting of the group and then use the meeting time to listen to the CD and discuss the lesson.

To ensure that everyone has a chance to participate in the discussion, the ideal size for a group is around eight to ten people. If there are more than ten people, try to break up the bigger group into smaller subgroups. Make sure the members are committed to participating each week, as this will help create stability and help you better prepare the structure of the meeting.

At the beginning of the study each week, start the session with a question to challenge group members to think about the issues you will be discussing. The members can answer briefly, but the goal is to have an idea in their mind as you go over the lesson. This allows the group members to become engaged and ready to interact with the group.

After reviewing the lesson, try to initiate a free-flowing discussion. Invite group members to bring questions and insights they may have discovered to the next meeting, especially if they were unsure of the meaning of some parts of the lesson. Be prepared to discuss how biblical truth applies to the world we live in today.

Weekly Preparation

As the group leader, here are a few things you can do to prepare for each meeting:

- Choose whether or not you will play the CD message during your small group session.

  If you decide to play the CD message from Dr. Jeremiah as part of the meeting, you will need to adjust the group time accordingly.

- Make sure you are thoroughly familiar with the material in the lesson.

  Make sure you understand the content of the lesson so you know how to structure group time and you are prepared to lead group discussion.

- Decide, ahead of time, which questions you plan to discuss.

  Depending on how much time you have each week, you may not be able to reflect on every question. Select specific questions which you feel will evoke the best discussion.

- Take prayer requests.

  At the end of your discussion, take prayer requests from your group members and pray for each other.

Structuring the Discussion Time

If you need help in organizing your time when planning your group Bible study, here are two schedules, for sixty minutes and ninety minutes, which can give you a structure for the lesson:

Option 1 (Listen to Audio CD)	60 Minutes	90 Minutes
Welcome: Members arrive and get settled.	N/A	5 minutes
Getting Started Question: Prepares the group for interacting with one another.	Welcome and Getting Started 5 minutes	15 minutes
Message: Listen to the audio CD.	40 minutes	40 minutes
Discussion: Discuss group study questions.	10 minutes	25 minutes
Prayer and Application: Final application for the week and prayer before dismissal.	5 minutes	5 minutes

Option 2 (No Audio CD)	60 Minutes	90 Minutes
Welcome: Members arrive and get settled.	5 minutes	10 minutes
Getting Started Question: Prepares the group for interacting with one another.	10 minutes	10 minutes
Message: Review the lesson.	15 minutes	25 minutes
Discussion: Discuss group study questions.	25 minutes	35 minutes
Prayer and Application: Final application for the week and prayer before dismissal.	5 minutes	10 minutes

As the group leader, it is up to you to keep track of the time and keep things moving along according to your schedule. If your group is having a good discussion, don't feel the need to stop and move on to the next question. Remember, the purpose is to pull together ideas, and share unique insights on the lesson. Make time each week to discuss how to apply these truths to living for Christ today.

The purpose of discussion is for everyone to participate, but don't be concerned if certain group members are more quiet—they may be internally reflecting on the questions and need time to process their ideas before they can share them.

Group Dynamics

Leading a group study can be a rewarding experience for you and your group members—but that doesn't mean there won't be challenges. Certain members may feel uncomfortable discussing topics that they consider very personal, and might be afraid of being called on. Some members might have disagreements on specific issues. To help prevent these scenarios, consider the following ground rules:

- If someone has a question that may seem off topic, suggest that it is discussed at another time, or ask the group if they are okay with addressing that topic.

- If someone asks a question you don't know the answer to, confess that you don't know and move on. If you feel comfortable, invite other group members to give their opinions, or share their comments based on personal experience.

- If you feel like a couple of people are talking much more than others, direct questions to people who may not have shared yet. You could even ask the more dominating members to help draw out the quiet ones.

- When there is a disagreement, encourage the group members to process the matter in love. Invite members from opposing sides to evaluate their opinions and consider the ideas of the other members. Lead the group through Scripture that addresses the topic, and look for common ground.

When issues arise, remind your group to think of Scripture: "Love one another" (John 13:34), "If it is possible, as much as depends on you, live peaceably with all men" (Romans 12:18), and "Be quick to listen, slow to speak and slow to become angry" (James 1:19, NIV).

For Continuing Study

For a complete listing of Dr. Jeremiah's materials for personal and group study call 1-800-947-1993, go online to www.DavidJeremiah.org, or write to Turning Point, P.O. Box 3838, San Diego, CA 92163.

Dr. Jeremiah's *Turning Point* program is currently heard or viewed around the world on radio, television, and the Internet in English. *Momento Decisivo*, the Spanish translation of Dr. Jeremiah's messages, can be heard on radio in every Spanish speaking country in the world. The television broadcast is also broadcast by satellite throughout the Middle East with Arabic subtitles.

Contact Turning Point for radio and television program times and stations in your area, or visit our website at www.DavidJeremiah.org/stationlocator.

THE GOD YOU MAY NOT KNOW

A man named Dennis Wise was a fan of Elvis Presley—a big fan. Not long after Presley died in 1977, Wise had a plastic surgeon reshape his face and his hairline so that his appearance bore a marked resemblance to Elvis. He went around impersonating the singer, picking up a few dollars here and there on the civic club circuit. When asked what motivated him to shape his life around that of Elvis Presley, Wise said the singer had been his role model—actually, his idol—for many years. Here are Wise's own words about his pursuit of all things Elvis, as reported in *The Boston Globe*:

> Presley's been an idol of mine ever since I was five years old. I have every record he ever made, twice over. Pictures in the thousands. I have books, magazines, pillows, even a couple of books in Chinese and Japanese about him. I even have tree leaves from the front of his house. I never saw Elvis Presley in person. I saw him in the movies four times. Once I stood up on the wall of the Presley mansion and tried to see him. For twelve hours I stood, trying to get a glimpse of him, but he had so many people around him that you would never get close.

It would be safe to say that Dennis Wise worshiped Elvis Presley—but he never met the object of his worship! Dennis Wise knew a lot about Elvis, but he didn't know the singer himself. Knowing all the hit songs, all the movie titles, all the concert appearances ... Elvis' personal preferences for food, clothes, cars ... none of that is the same as knowing the singer himself.

And therein lies a valuable lesson for Christians: Knowing about God, the object of our worship, is not the same as knowing God Himself.

Facts and figures are lifeless. So are books and articles and social media. They may provide an introduction to the person we admire, but they cannot replace a relationship with the person. Better to know about a person than to know nothing at all. But a relationship never becomes the intimate exchange it should be until there is a personal encounter—hand-to-hand, face-to-face, and heart-to-heart.

Many Christians know a lot about God. They have read books, even read the Bible, and may have attended church for years and—don't get me wrong—I am for all those things. Gathering accurate information about God is often where we start in our relationship with Him. But if our relationship never moves to the place of spiritual worship ... if we remain a repository of facts and figures, then we live out our lives as academic Christians, not actual Christians. The heart of the Christian experience is worship of our Creator-God, and here's how we get to that place: We can only worship someone we love, and we can only love someone we know.

Do you know about God, or do you know Him? *The God You May Not Know* has the ultimate goal of encouraging you to know God with your whole heart. It's based on the Bible, a living book (Hebrews 4:12). In its pages you will encounter the living and true God who will reveal Himself to you for who He is: a holy, faithful, eternal, changeless, powerful, good, all-knowing, sovereign, ever-present, and loving God.

You may already know a lot about God, and even know Him personally. But I invite you not to be content with where you are with Him. Meet Him, know Him, love Him, and worship Him for who He is.

KNOWING THE GOD YOU WORSHIP

Jeremiah 9:23-24

*In this lesson we discover the benefits
of knowing the one, true God.*

OUTLINE

In a world of superficial relationships and facts masquerading as knowledge, it's easy to treat God as a commodity. We learn certain bits of information about Him and call it "knowing God." But we can only worship someone we love, and we can only love someone we truly know.

I.   Knowing God Gives a Sense of Pride

II. Knowing God Gives a Sense of Purpose

III. Knowing God Gives a Sense of Power

IV. Knowing God Gives a Sense of Peace

I have a special place in the mountains near where I live that I consider "my place." It's not, of course—it's public property that anyone can visit. But I got in the habit of going there a while back when I was going through a difficult period in my life—health challenges, the outcome of which was not always certain. I needed a place to go to pray and think and listen for God's leading in my heart during that time.

While spending time alone with God at my place, I have pondered the question of what it means to know Him. Not to know about God, but to *really* know Him. I think most Christians feel a distance from God that they can't really explain, a sense that, if God is really God and they are really His children, knowing Him ought to be something more than it is. And those of us who are involved in ministry vocationally— "professional" Christians, if you will—suffer from a different problem. We have made a science out of knowing God. We've been taught and trained to know Him, mostly with our intellect, so we face a constant challenge of breaking through the veneer of professionalism and entering into a worshipful relationship with God based on knowing Him intimately.

Here is the conclusion I have come to in my own thoughts on knowing God: We can only worship someone we love, and we can only love someone we know.

Worship, therefore, begins with a heart that has touched the heart of God, a heart that truly knows the one we worship. If we come to know Him as He wants to be known, we will love Him. And if we love Him, worship will not be something we "do" as much as it will flow naturally from a heart filled with the knowledge of and love for God. Worship is an uncontrolled release of expression from a heart that can't contain its love for God.

Consider your own relationship with your spouse or sweetheart. If the extent of that relationship was the exchange of a gift of flowers or chocolates or other remembrances on a regular basis, but no personal communication to go along with it, what kind of relationship would it be? No relationship will prosper if it is based solely on "things" without an accompanying revelation of the heart and soul.

But is that how we treat God? We bring Him flowers and chocolates once a week in the form of our tithes and offerings or our presence in the church's weekly meetings. And then we wonder why our relationship with Him doesn't grow. If that's how we seek to develop a relationship with God, some serious problems will, in time, arise.

First, if we don't really know the true God, we will be tempted to create a god who is convenient for us, one who doesn't infringe on our ideas of what the Christian life should be. An article by James Edwards in *Discipleship Journal* illustrates this danger. After speaking to a conference of Christian singles, the subject of sexual ethics came up in the question-and-answer session following his talk.

Asked to share what I believed the Bible taught on the subject, it was my understanding the Bible taught fidelity within marriage and abstinence outside of it. When I finished, a man challenged what I had said and he said he did not believe in a God who would impose those kinds of limitations or even penalties on the experience of sex. He then proceeded to tell me and the group what kind of god he did believe in— a god of love and not law, as he called it. He succeeded in the next few moments in putting into words something many people want to believe, although not many would be as brave as he was to try to say it publicly.

The man didn't know the true God (or at least didn't like God's ethical standards on sex), so he invented his own god, one who would agree with his views.

When you think about it, this is almost comical—that we would attempt to define who God is on the basis of our own whims and desires. God is God and is not affected at all by who we think He is or should be. But if we don't commit ourselves to knowing Him as He is, we will soon find that the God we worship bears little resemblance to the God of Scripture. For too many Christians, theology is determined by practice: We decide what we want to do, then invent a theology that allows it.

Second, if we don't know the true God for who He really is, we become vulnerable to someone else telling us who God is. I have seen many times in counseling where Christians have a difficult time knowing God because of abuses by their own father when they were young. They can't disconnect their knowledge of their earthly father from their knowledge of their Heavenly Father, and so never come to know Him for who He is. All of us are affected one way or another by our earthly fathers, but this can't be a lifelong excuse for failing to come to know the true God.

While those dangers are real, there are also four powerful things that happen when we come to know God in an intimate way. I trust these four positive benefits will encourage you to pursue Him through the remainder of the lessons in this series on knowing the God you worship.

KNOWING GOD GIVES A SENSE OF PRIDE

Jeremiah 9:23-24 says,

"Let not the wise man glory in his wisdom,
Let not the mighty man glory in his might,
Nor let the rich man glory in his riches;
But let him who glories glory in this,
That he understands and knows Me,
That I am the Lord, exercising
    lovingkindness, judgment, and
    righteousness in the earth.
For in these I delight," says the Lord.

In what do you boast or brag? Money? Intelligence? Popularity? Wisdom? Accomplishments? Jeremiah says don't boast about any of those things. Boasting is not wrong as long as we boast in the right thing: that we understand and know God. We find more than one person in the Bible boasting about knowing Him.

The apostle Paul would boast in nothing except "the cross of our Lord Jesus Christ" (Galatians 6:14). Hosea the prophet wrote that God delights more in people knowing Him than in making sacrifices to Him (Hosea 6:6). Worship is important, but knowing God is the most important thing of all.

When Paul was in prison in Rome, writing to the church in Philippi, he said that the ultimate purpose of his life could be summarized this way: "that I may know Him and the power of His resurrection, and the fellowship of His sufferings, being conformed to His death" (Philippians 3:10). When you read Paul's letters, it is easy to see that this one thing was the focus of his entire life; it was his passion and reason for living.

Paul also writes that every Christian will one day "know just as I also am known" (1 Corinthians 13:12). That will require a serious adjustment for many Christians, but it shouldn't. We ought to know God so well when we die that our transition to heaven goes off without a hitch. A speaker at the funeral service of Dr. Raymond Edmund, former president of Wheaton College, said, "Ray Edmund's translation to glory will be the smoothest thing that ever happened" in the history of people entering heaven. That is, his knowledge of God was so intimate while on earth that his adjustment to knowing and being known fully in heaven would be minimal—just a different location.

KNOWING GOD GIVES A SENSE OF PURPOSE

In a wonderful passage in 1 John 2:12-14, the apostle Paul describes stages of spiritual growth and maturity that believers go through. There are spiritual "children," "young men," and "fathers."

Spiritual children are those whose "sins are forgiven." They are people who don't know any more than that they are born again and have eternal life. Some people have been Christians for ten or twenty years but are still spiritual children. They don't know anything about Christian truth or doctrine, and they don't know much about God. Spiritual infancy, just like physical infancy, is to be expected. But it should transition into the next phase at the appropriate time.

Becoming a spiritual young man, or adolescent in the faith, should follow infancy. This is the time when your faith is tested and you must prove what you believe. You begin to learn truth about God and see it validated in your own experience; you win more spiritual battles than you lose.

Then you become a spiritual adult, or a "father," because "you have known Him who is from the beginning." There is a big gap between being a spiritual child and young man, but an even larger gap between being a young man and a father. Why? Because being a spiritual adult means you move from knowing about God to knowing Him personally.

Where are you on John's continuum of spiritual growth and maturity? If all you know is that you're saved, you need to take it to the next level. If you're a spiritual adolescent, you need to focus on knowing God. This is not a matter of pride but a matter of purpose in our lives so that we ultimately come to know God, not just know about Him.

KNOWING GOD GIVES A SENSE OF POWER

In Daniel 11:32 we read that those "who know their God shall be strong, and carry out great exploits." Daniel was an unwilling resident of Babylon when he wrote those words, having been taken there in the exile of Jews from Jerusalem. He was in a setting where his faith was opposed by the culture around him. But he found strength in his knowledge of God.

When he first arrived in Babylon as a prisoner, he was chosen to serve in the king's court. When told he must eat from the king's dining room, which would violate his Jewish dietary standards, he refused.

Daniel knew his God and gained strength from his covenant commitment to honor God's Word. Daniel and his three friends were the only Jewish hostages mentioned as standing firm instead of violating their conscience and God's standards (Daniel 1).

Daniel's three friends found themselves in yet another challenging spot when they refused to bow down before the statue of King Nebuchadnezzar. When the king heard about their refusal, he was furious and threatened to throw them into a furnace of fire. Their answer to the king went like this: "Our God whom we serve is able to deliver us from the burning fiery furnace, and He will deliver us from your hand, O king. But if not, let it be known to you, O king, that we do not serve your gods, nor will we worship the gold image which you have set up" (Daniel 3:17-18). Whenever I read this account, I am encouraged to know God better because I want that kind of power in my own life!

Christians are guilty of playing the role of victims—we live with a mentality of being the persecuted victims in this world. But we are not victims—we are the victors! And knowing God will give us the power to live like it. Those young Hebrews in Babylon could stand up to the king because they knew God and knew they were in the center of His will. They weren't afraid of anything or anyone, and were not about to defile their consciences or lower their standards just to please a pagan king. Maybe if we knew God as well as those young Hebrew men did, we would live with that same fearless power.

KNOWING GOD GIVES A SENSE OF PEACE

It's easy to read the paper and watch the news on television and fall into a sense of despair about conditions in this world. We wonder if God really is in control. We find out in Daniel that Nebuchadnezzar discovered who is really in charge of the affairs of this world. In Daniel 4, the king had a dream that he called upon Daniel to interpret for him. The essence of the interpretation was that God was going to depose the king for a period of seven years, during which time he would act like an animal, grazing on the grass of the field. At the end of the seven years, Nebuchadnezzar made a statement about what he had learned in his crash course about who's really in charge in the world: "I blessed the Most High and praised and honored Him who lives forever: For His dominion is an everlasting dominion, and His kingdom is from generation to generation. All the inhabitants of the earth are reputed as nothing; He does according to His will in the army of heaven and among the inhabitants of the earth. No one can restrain His hand or say to Him, 'What have You done?'" (Daniel 4:34-35)

Nebuchadnezzar, who had maintained a lofty view and opinion of his role and influence in the world, had come to understand who truly is in charge. After being humbled by God for seven years, there was no question in his mind about the power of God to work out His will. He learned that God is in charge.

When we know who our God is and transfer our head knowledge to a level of trust, we can live in peace. We can sleep soundly at night and not worry about what we read in the paper that day. We learn that His sovereignty, holiness, justice, omnipotence, and omniscience will guard us daily. But if we don't know Him, the affairs of this world will keep us in a constant state of fear and anxiety.

The prophet Daniel foretold a time when God will establish His kingdom on the earth and destroy all other earthly kingdoms in the process. The certainty of that future reality should also translate into a certainty about the present day. Just as God knows the future, He knows the present as well. There is nothing you are experiencing that He is not fully aware of. God is never taken by surprise, and He never goes on vacation. There is no reason for you not to live in perfect peace when you know your God.

Do you know God or just know about God? That answer can be determined by the sense of pride, purpose, power, and peace that others see in your life. When we know Him, not only are we prepared to live each day, but we are preparing ourselves for a seamless transition into eternity: "And this is eternal life, that they may know You, the only true God, and Jesus Christ whom You have sent" (John 17:3).

PERSONAL QUESTIONS

1. Have you ever seen examples of people creating their own god to fit what they want?

   a. If so, in what areas do they compromise God?

   b. What happens if we don't know the true God for who He really is?

2. Read Jeremiah 9:23-24.

   a. What does the Lord say He delights in?

   b. Is it wrong to boast? If not, what should we boast in?

   c. What was Paul's ultimate purpose in life? (See Philippians 3:10.)

3. Turn to 1 John 2:12-14.

   a. List and describe the three stages of spiritual maturity that John mentions.

      •

      •

      •

   b. Where do you think you are on the ladder of spiritual maturity?

4. Daniel knew God and was unwilling to break his commitment to Him.

   a. In Daniel 11:32, what does Daniel say will happen to those who know God?

   b. What did Shadrach, Meshach, and Abed-Nego tell King Nebuchadnezzar after he threatened to throw them into a fiery furnace? (Daniel 3:18)

   c. The young Hebrew men knew their God so well that they had fearless power. Have there been moments in your life when you knew God's power and became fearless in the face of opposition?

1. Read Jeremiah 9:23-24 as a group.

   a. In what does the Lord delight?

   b. What are we not to boast about? What should we boast in instead?

   c. What did the apostle Paul boast in? (See Galatians 6:14.)

2. Turn to 1 John 2:12-14.

   a. As a group, list and describe the three stages of spiritual maturity that John mentions.

      •

      •

      •

   b. If comfortable, share with the group where you are on the ladder of spiritual maturity.

   c. What can you do in order to reach the next level of maturity?

   d. How is the apostle Paul a great example of spiritual maturity?

3. Read Daniel 11:32 together.

   a. What happens to those who know God?

   b. What happened to Daniel and his three friends when they stood firm against violating God's standards? (Daniel 1)

4. Go to the section titled, "Knowing God Gives a Sense of Peace."

   a. What can we learn about God as we begin to know Him more and more?

   b. If we don't know Him, what will happen?

5. Based on this lesson, do you firmly believe that you know God? Or do you just know about God? If comfortable, share with the group.

DID YOU KNOW?

The humbling condition Nebuchadnezzar experienced—living life as if a beast of the field—may have been a condition known as lycanthropy. From the Greek *lykos* (wolf) and *anthropos* (man), lycanthropy is a mental disorder in which a person believes himself to be a wolf or some other nonhuman animal. From ancient times, people have been known to take on the characteristics of the most dangerous beast of prey in their geographical region of the world. The disorder is linked with a belief in animal guardian spirits, vampires, totemism, witches, and werewolves. Many nations have instances of lycanthropy in their folklore and legends. While Nebuchadnezzar's seven-year bout might have been explained clinically as lycanthropy, it was brought on, and ended, by the supernatural intervention of God as a device to humble a prideful world ruler.

KNOWING
A HOLY GOD

Revelation 15:4

*In this lesson we learn what it means
that God is holy.*

OUTLINE

There's probably no one who hasn't used the word *holy* as part of a slang expression in conversation (what does "holy cow" mean, anyway?). The next time you catch yourself saying "holy [whatever]," remember there is One who truly is holy, set apart from all that is not.

 I.   **Moses' Experience of the Holy**

 II. **Job's Experience of the Holy**

 III. **Isaiah's Experience of the Holy**

 IV. **Paul's Experience of the Holy**

 V.   **John's Experience of the Holy**

 VI. **Our Experience of the Holy**
     A. We Will See Ourselves as We Really Are
     B. We Will Understand the Cross
     C. We Will Worship Him
     D. We Will Cultivate the Habit of Holiness
     E. We Will Be Like Him

It's a shame when words that have strong spiritual connotations become part of the slang language of a culture. Take the word *holy*, for instance; and think of all the ways it's used that detract from its original meaning: "holy cow," "holy smoke," "holy Joe," "holy mackerel," "holy Toledo," and "holy roller." I'm sure there are reasons, but I can't imagine what *holy* has to do with most of those words. All I know is that when an important word like *holy* is used as slang, people stop wondering what it means—it's just an expression.

Even Christians have lost touch with the concept of holiness. Esteemed theologian J. I. Packer has written, "To listen to our sermons, and to read the books we write for each other, and then to watch the zany, worldly, quarrelsome way we behave as Christian people, you would never imagine that once the highway of holiness was clearly marked out for Bible believers so that ministers and people knew what it was and could speak of it with authority and confidence." Many Christians view God as a lenient grandfather who winks at our indiscretions from His rocking chair in heaven.

Church history reveals that every major revival in the history of the Church was sparked and fueled by the concept of the holiness of God. Great Church leaders like John Wesley, Andrew Murray, F. B. Meyer, Oswald Chambers, and Amy Carmichael kept the holiness of God at the center of their ministries and writings.

In this study on knowing the God you worship, we will be looking at many of the attributes of God. We begin with the holiness of God because it is the fundamental attribute of God. God is called "holy" in Scripture more than anything else. Someone has said that His arm of power tells us of His strength, His eye of omniscience tells us of His knowledge, and His heart of duration tells us of His eternity. But it is the beauty of His holiness that captures us when we really see Him as He is. The holiness of God, according to the Scripture, is His beauty. Nearly every book of the Bible touches on the holiness of God in some way (Exodus 15:11; Leviticus 19:2; 1 Samuel 2:2; Psalm 22:3).

In order to regain a proper understanding of the holiness of God, we need to understand this biblical term. Holiness involves a range of meaning perhaps best summarized in the idea of complete purity and goodness: the absence of anything dark or sinful or evil at all (1 John 1:5). But there is more to holiness than the presence of purity and the absence of evil. *Holy* comes from a word that means "to cut apart" or "set apart." Therefore, holiness refers to something that is separate, not attached to, or different from. God is like a foreign being compared to the sinful nature of humanity. He is totally set apart and different in His nature.

Early in the twentieth century, a German scholar named Rudolf Otto went around the world studying the concept of "holy" in different cultures. Wherever he went, he discovered that people found it difficult to describe what *holy* meant. They could sense it, and they knew it when they saw or experienced it, but they couldn't find words to describe it. The most common theme he heard was that, rather than describing *holy*, they described their own "creatureliness" whenever they found themselves in the presence of the holy. They could sense their own finiteness, their own lack of purity, their own smallness when in the presence of the holy. That's how it is when we are in the presence of our holy God—we know better who we are compared to Him.

In the Bible we have the accounts of several individuals who found themselves in the presence of the holy. They didn't define *holy*, but their responses provide clues to what it means.

MOSES' EXPERIENCE OF THE HOLY

Before the Exodus, Moses found himself on holy ground when he encountered the burning bush on Mount Horeb (Exodus 3). Later, Moses had another experience with the holiness of God that is not as well known.

After the Exodus, Moses was on the same mountain receiving the Law from God when he made an unusual request of God: "Please, show me Your glory" (Exodus 33:18). You might think that Moses had seen plenty in Egypt—the plagues, the Passover, the crossing of the Red Sea—but that wasn't enough. He wanted to see more; he wanted to see God's glory, His face. He didn't get to see the face of God, His full glory, but God gave him an approximate experience. He promised to pass by in front of Moses, shielding Moses' view with His hand, then remove His hand as He passed by so Moses could see His back.

It was a good thing Moses did not see the full glory of God, or he would have died. As it was, when he came down off the mountain, the people were afraid of him because his face shone. His face was aglow with the reflected glory of God (Exodus 34:29-30). He ultimately had to cover his face with a veil because no one would come near him otherwise (verse 33).

Even a partial revelation of the glory of God transformed Moses and was immediately visible to everyone around him.

JOB'S EXPERIENCE OF THE HOLY

After Job went through his own life-changing experience of suffering, he experienced a revelation of God that changed him even further. At the end of the book of Job, we read his response to what he learned about God: "I have heard of You by the hearing of the ear, but now my eye sees You. Therefore I abhor myself, and repent in dust and ashes" (Job 42:5-6). Earlier he had said, "Behold, I am vile; what shall I answer You? I lay my hand over my mouth" (Job 40:4).

Job found himself too unworthy even to speak in God's presence. Seeing the holiness and power of God renders those who see Him speechless.

ISAIAH'S EXPERIENCE OF THE HOLY

Isaiah's experience of the holy was perhaps the most dramatic of all who encountered God (Isaiah 6). God called Isaiah in the year that King Uzziah died, a great king in Israel who had reigned for 52 years. Uzziah served God faithfully until near the end of his reign when, in a moment of pride and arrogance, he usurped the role of priest in the temple, which was an offense to God. As a result, Uzziah broke out in leprosy, which meant he had to be quarantined away from the people, where he died. When he died, the whole nation mourned because he had been a righteous king up until that final mistake at the end of his life.

During that year, as Isaiah was at the temple to seek the Lord's guidance for Israel in the absence of her king, he saw the Lord "sitting on a throne, high and lifted up, and the train of His robe filled the temple" (Isaiah 6:1). The seraphim who attended the Lord cried out, "Holy, holy, holy is the Lord of hosts; the whole earth is full of His glory!" (verse 3) In response, Isaiah cried out, "Woe is me, for I am undone! Because I am a man of unclean lips . . . for my eyes have seen the King, the Lord of hosts" (verse 5). One of the seraphim then took a live coal from the altar and touched Isaiah's lips and said, "Your iniquity is taken away, and your sin purged" (verse 7).

In the Hebrew culture and language, repetition of words was used for emphasis (like Jesus saying, "Verily, verily" [KJV] or "truly, truly" [NASB] when He wanted to emphasize what He was about to say). Triplicates were rare, and signified intense emphasis, as when the angels cried, "Holy, holy, holy is the Lord of hosts." We don't find "loving, loving, loving" or "gracious, gracious, gracious" in the Bible, but we do find "holy, holy, holy"—the only attribute of God repeated three times for emphasis.

And Isaiah's response was like everyone else's—a profound sense of unworthiness. *Undone* means "disintegrated." He lost all sense of his own wholeness in the presence of the holiness of God.

PAUL'S EXPERIENCE OF THE HOLY

Saul of Tarsus (his name before becoming the apostle Paul) was traveling from Jerusalem to Damascus to find and persecute Christians (Acts 9:1-16; 22:1-21; 26:9-18). As he traveled, a bright light from heaven appeared and Paul fell to the ground in response. Though he didn't realize it immediately, Paul was being confronted by the risen and living Christ in all His glory. Paul was temporarily blinded by the experience, but was ultimately converted to faith in Christ. When he saw the glory of the Person he had been persecuting, Paul succumbed to that glory with all his life and became the greatest of the apostles.

Paul's encounter with the glory of God is perhaps the most life-changing instance recorded in Scripture.

JOHN'S EXPERIENCE OF THE HOLY

When the apostle John was given the opportunity to look into heaven, he saw the enthroned Lord. In Revelation 1, John describes the awesome appearance of the Lord Jesus Christ and then says, "When I saw Him, I fell at His feet as dead" (verse 17). John's experience was not unlike the experience of others when they saw the glory of God.

Rudolf Otto was right! The consistent response to being in the presence of the holiness of God is an immediate realization of one's own unworthiness. Job put his hand over his mouth; Isaiah saw his sinfulness; Saul fell to the ground; John fell down as if he were dead. After seeing these responses, I am surer than ever that none of us has really experienced the holiness of God. We humans—including we who are Christians—are a profane people. If we ever saw our holy God, we would know it like never before.

What should our response be to what we learn from these men's experiences with the holiness of God?

OUR EXPERIENCE OF THE HOLY

The more clearly we understand God's holiness, the more the following will be true of us.

We Will See Ourselves as We Really Are

The more we see of God's holiness, the more we see of our unholiness—our own "creatureliness." Romans 3:23 says, "All have sinned and fall short of the glory of God." The more we understand God's holiness, the more we will agree that we have fallen short of it.

As long as we fall short, we can never expect to have fellowship with God on the basis of our own lives. The best we can offer Him is the equivalent of "filthy rags" (Isaiah 64:6). This is the bad news we have to understand before the Good News of the Gospel makes sense. My father, who was a preacher, used to say when I was growing up, "Before you can get some people saved, you have to get them 'un-saved.'" He meant, of course, that they have to see their own unrighteousness before they can see their need for a Savior. God's holiness is the only standard for what is acceptable to Him, and we cannot achieve that standard on our own.

We Will Understand the Cross

Once we see who we are compared to who God is, we understand the Cross of Christ.

I'm not sure we truly understand the Cross as well as we should. God the Father killed His own Son! Why did He do that? It all has to do with holiness. If we don't understand holiness, we won't understand the Cross.

Christ came into the world to provide sinful people with access to a holy God. If Christ had not died for our unholiness, we would have remained in our sins and been barred forever from the presence of a holy God. We know our sins were actually upon Christ because God, in His holiness, could not even look upon His own Son on the cross who now carried upon Himself the sins of the world. He forsook His own Son in order that we might be made holy in Christ.

What Christ accomplished on the cross was to weave a new suit of clothes for you and me to wear that we might be clothed with His own holiness. So now, when God looks at me, He does not see my sin but the holiness of His Son in which I am clothed. That is the purpose of the Cross—to provide that which the holiness of God demanded. God took the life of His own Son instead of our lives, and He gave us Christ's righteousness in exchange.

We Will Worship Him

There is a definite connection between seeing God's holiness and worship (Psalm 30:4; 89:7; 99:5). Worship is more a verb than a noun, something we actively accomplish, not passively observe. All the biblical characters I cited earlier in this lesson worshiped God when they saw His holiness. But when we see God's holiness, we do more than participate in worship on Sunday. Our whole life becomes an act of worship. Our money, our jobs, our hobbies, our recreation—everything becomes an offering of worship to Him (Romans 12:1).

We Will Cultivate the Habit of Holiness

When we see God's holiness, we are motivated to become holy ourselves. First Peter says in several ways that because God is holy, we likewise ought to be holy (1:15; 2:5, 9). We cannot be as holy as God, but we are to set ourselves apart from this world as He is set apart; as He is holy, we are to be holy. There used to be a doctrine in the Christian Church in America called "separation," which emphasized the believer's separateness from the world. That can easily become a kind of legalism, but the idea was right. We are to be holy unto the Lord, set apart from the world.

We Will Be Like Him

When we see God's holiness, it makes us long for the day when we will be like Him. Even though I will never be as holy as Christ in this life, the day is coming when "we shall be like Him, for we shall see Him as He is" (1 John 3:2). We will become as beautiful as Christ Himself, beauty being defined as the absence of sin and therefore the reality of holiness.

I hope you are looking forward to the day when you will see Christ and be like Him. That all begins with seeing your need for His Cross, your need to swap your unholiness for His holiness. That is a step you can take today by putting your faith in Christ for the forgiveness of your sins.

1. Read 1 John 1:5.

   a. How is the holiness of God described in this verse?

   b. What does it mean to be "holy"?

2. Read Exodus 33:18-23.

   a. After Moses received the law from God on Mount Horeb, what did he ask of God? (verse 18)

   b. How did God respond? (verses 19-23)

   c. What would have happened to Moses if he saw God's face? (verse 20)

3. An encounter with the holiness of God has a tremendous impact. Isaiah had a dramatic experience when he encountered God's holiness. Read Isaiah 6:1-5.

   a. In Isaiah 6:1, what did Isaiah see in the year King Uzziah died?

   b. Who was in attendance with the Lord? What word was cried out three times? (verses 2-3)

   c. Explain the importance of the repetition found in the seraphim's words. (verse 3)

   d. What was Isaiah's response? (verse 5)

4. Turn to the section titled, "Our Experience of the Holy."

   a. According to Romans 3:23, what prevents us from experiencing the fullness of God's glory?

   b. In Isaiah 64:6, what is our righteousness compared to?

   c. What would the result of our life be if Christ had not died for our unholiness?

1. Read 1 John 1:5 together.

   a. How is God's holiness described?

   b. Based on this lesson, what does it mean to be "holy"? Discuss.

   c. How does our modern world describe being "holy"? Share your thoughts with the group.

2. We studied the lives of five biblical men and their experience of the holy. Together, compare and contrast those experiences below.

   a. Moses

   b. Job

   c. Isaiah

   d. Paul

   e. John

3. From this lesson, is there an experience of the holy that you can identify with? Why or why not?

4. According to Romans 3:23, what prevents us from experiencing the fullness of God's glory?

5. Read Psalm 30:4, 89:7, and 99:5 as a group.

   a. What connection can be made between God's holiness and worship?

   b. How should we live our life in response to the holiness of God? (1 Peter 1:15)

6. As we see more of God's holiness in our life, what do we also begin to see? How does seeing God's holiness help us to better understand the Cross? Explain your answer to the group.

DID YOU KNOW?

The New Testament word "saint" is an English translation of the Greek word *hagios*, which means "holy." Therefore, in New Testament terms, a saint is a holy one. There is a dual aspect to sainthood: We are holy before God, but we are to become holy in practice. Christians are called "holy" (that is, saints) in Romans 1:7; 1 Corinthians 1:2; 2 Corinthians 1:1; Ephesians 1:1; Philippians 1:1; and Colossians 1:2. But we are also told to be holy in our lifestyles— essentially, to live a life of moral and ethical purity, free from sin (Matthew 5:8; 23:26; Romans 12:1; 1 Timothy 1:5; 2 Timothy 2:22; Titus 1:15; James 1:27). The Christian's purity of position in God's sight is to lead to a purity of practice. The fellowship between Christians was viewed as a holy calling, illustrated by the greeting known as the "holy kiss" in the first-century churches (1 Corinthians 16:20; 2 Corinthians 13:12; 1 Thessalonians 5:26).

KNOWING
A FAITHFUL GOD

Lamentations 3:22-23

*In this lesson we learn the difference God's
faithfulness makes in our lives.*

OUTLINE

Every marriage vow that is not kept, every promise that is not fulfilled,
every debt that is not paid, and every promised prayer that is not prayed…
all touch on the issue of faithfulness. If there is anything humans are,
it is unfaithful. And if there is anything God is, thankfully, it is faithful.

  I.   **Because God Is Faithful, We Can Have Confidence
When We Pray**

  II. **Because God Is Faithful, We Can Conquer Evil and Temptation**

 III. **Because God Is Faithful, We Can Praise Him**

 IV. **Because God Is Faithful, We Can Have Courage When
We Are Afraid**

There was a time in our country when business was done on the basis of a promise and a handshake, when "'til death do us part" meant exactly that, and when promises made were promises kept. But the condition we find ourselves in today is not a new one. Solomon asked centuries ago, "Who can find a faithful man?" (Proverbs 20:6)

There is still One whose word is His bond, One who can be completely trusted in everything, One who is faithful in all things, and One who is not changed by time or circumstance. Part of God's character is His faithfulness, and we worship Him for it.

None of the things that cause men and women today to be unfaithful ever impact God: selfish desire, fear, weakness, loss of interest, strong temptation. Those things cause us to be unfaithful—not God. Numbers 23:19 says, "God is not a man, that He should lie," or do anything else men do. God's "compassions fail not. They are new every morning; great is [His] faithfulness" (Lamentations 3:22-23).

In the Old Testament, "faithful" comes from the Hebrew root *aman*, from which we get our word *amen*. The root meant "to confirm, support," and *amen* means "so be it." Every one of God's promises are "amen"—confirmed and certain. Jesus Christ is also called "the Amen" in Revelation 3:14. "Faithful" in the New Testament is *pistos* and is used fifteen times to describe God. From Genesis to Revelation, God is a faithful God.

Psalm 119:90 says, "Your faithfulness endures to all generations." And after the Flood, God told Noah, "While the earth remains, seedtime and harvest, cold and heat, winter and summer, and day and night shall not cease" (Genesis 8:22). And they haven't! God's faithfulness stands at the very heart of His creation.

But God's faithfulness is also at the core of His revelation in His Word. To be faithful means to stand behind your word, to remain constant in spite of circumstances. Deuteronomy 7:9 says, "Therefore know that the Lord your God, He is God, the faithful God who keeps covenant." God's faithfulness to His Word is found in Joshua's farewell words to Israel: "And you know in all your hearts and in all your souls that not one thing has failed of all the good things which the Lord your God spoke concerning you. All have come to pass for you; not one word of them has failed" (Joshua 23:14). Joshua had experienced the faithfulness of God to keep His covenant promises to Israel.

In this series we will identify God's attributes which lead us to worship Him and how those attributes impact our life. What does God's faithfulness mean to us?

Because God Is Faithful, We Can Have Confidence When We Pray

In Psalm 143:1, the psalmist prays, "Hear my prayer, O Lord, give ear to my supplications! In Your faithfulness answer me, and in Your righteousness." His words reflect his knowledge that God was faithful to answer prayers in the past. So he asks God to be faithful now. God tells us to call upon Him (Psalm 50:15; 91:15; Jeremiah 29:12) because He is faithful to hear and answer our prayers. Because He is faithful, we pray with confidence.

Because God Is Faithful, We Can Conquer Evil and Temptation

Second Thessalonians 3:3 says, "But the Lord is faithful, who will establish you and guard you from the evil one." Pray the Lord's Prayer, "And do not lead us into temptation, but deliver us from the evil one" (Matthew 6:13), and God will answer, "I am faithful. I will guard your steps." Or trust in 1 Corinthians 10:13, "No temptation has overtaken you except such as is common to man; but God is faithful, who will not allow you to be tempted beyond what you are able, but with the temptation will also make the way of escape, that you may be able to bear it."

When we face temptation, we must remember that God is faithful. He has promised to keep us from the evil one by providing a way of escape in every case. He is always faithful to provide a way of escape. God's name and character are at stake.

When we think of God's faithfulness, we might think of what we aren't in light of what He is. That is, we think of our own unfaithfulness when we think of God's faithfulness. Second Timothy 2:13 says, "If we are faithless, He remains faithful; He cannot deny Himself." No one who has been unfaithful should forget that God remains faithful even when we are not. If we confess our sins, He is faithful to forgive us and cleanse us from all unrighteousness (1 John 1:9).

There is no limit to the forgiveness and faithfulness of God. We think there must be because there is with us. We get tired of forgiving and being faithful, but God does not. He remains faithful even when we do not.

Because God Is Faithful, We Can Praise Him

In his book *Reflections on the Psalms*, C. S. Lewis says this about praise:

The most obvious fact about praise—whether of God or anything, strangely had escaped me. I thought of it in terms of compliment,

approval, or the giving of honor. I had never noticed that all enjoyment spontaneously overflows into praise....The world rings with praise...readers [praising] their favorite poet, walkers praising the countryside, players praising their favorite game—even praise of weather...dishes...actors...flowers, mountains, rare stamps, even politicians or scholars. I had not noticed how the humblest and at the same time most balanced...minds praised most, while the cranks, misfits, and malcontents praised least....
I had not noticed either that just as men spontaneously praise whatever they value, so they spontaneously urge us in joining them in praising it. "Isn't she lovely?" "Wasn't it glorious?" "Don't you think it magnificent?" The psalmists in telling everyone to praise God are doing what all men do when they speak of what they care about....I think we delight to praise what we enjoy because the praise not merely expresses but completes the enjoyment.[1]

I find it far more enjoyable to watch sports on TV with someone else than by myself. I'll often call Donna into the room to watch a replay of a particularly great play. It's just more fun to encourage others to join in praise with me.

Praise is the consummation of enjoyment. When we really enjoy a person, thing, or event, the experience remains incomplete until we offer up our praise. When the psalmist enjoins his readers to praise God with him, he is saying, "Isn't God great? I just want to lift up His praise. Would you praise Him with me? Isn't He lovely? Wasn't that magnificent? Isn't this incredible?" And there is no facet of God's nature that is lifted up for praise in Psalms more than His faithfulness:

Psalm 89:1:

I will sing of the mercies of the Lord forever;
With my mouth will I make known Your faithfulness
   to all generations.

Psalm 89:5:

And the heavens will praise Your wonders, O Lord;
Your faithfulness also in the assembly of the saints.

Psalm 89:8:

O Lord God of hosts,
Who is mighty like You, O Lord?
Your faithfulness also surrounds You.

I challenge you to read through the Psalms and underline every time you are encouraged or exhorted to praise God for one of His attributes—especially His faithfulness. And then enter into that praise in your own devotional time. Until we praise Him, the loop remains unclosed, and our complete enjoyment of God remains unfulfilled.

BECAUSE GOD IS FAITHFUL, WE CAN HAVE COURAGE WHEN WE ARE AFRAID

Lamentations has one of the key verses on God's faithfulness in all the Bible. To understand this verse, we have to understand the book of Lamentations; some have called it the "weepings" of Jeremiah, or Jeremiah's funeral poem.

Jeremiah was a prophet of God whose ministry took place when the city of Jerusalem was besieged and ultimately destroyed by the Babylonians. It must have been horrible for a godly prophet to watch the city of God be destroyed in judgment for the sins of the people. Lamentations was written through the tears of the prophet as he lamented the devastation of God's chosen city and her people.

Jerusalem had been under siege for eighteen months. People were dying of starvation and thirst, the normal result of ancient warfare sieges on a city: cut off their supplies and wait until the people die or are too weak to defend themselves. It got so bad in Jerusalem that people were killing and eating their own children to stay alive (Lamentations 4:10).

Lamentations 1:1-2 records Jeremiah's words as he looks out over the devastated city of Jerusalem:

How lonely sits the city
That was full of people!
How like a widow is she,
Who was great among the nations!
The princess among the provinces
Has become a slave!
She weeps bitterly in the night,
Her tears are on her cheeks;
Among all her lovers
She has none to comfort her.
All her friends have dealt treacherously with her;
They have become her enemies.

Understandably, Jeremiah reacted angrily toward God for what He had allowed to happen to Jerusalem. But ultimately his lament became personal: "Why have you allowed this to happen to me?"

Note his words in 1:12:

Is it nothing to you, all you who pass by?
Behold and see
If there is any sorrow like my sorrow,
Which has been brought on me,
Which the Lord has inflicted
In the day of His fierce anger.

And verse 16:

> For these things I weep;
> My eye, my eye overflows with water;
> Because the comforter, who should restore my life,
> Is far from me.
> My children are desolate
> Because the enemy prevailed.

Lamentations 3 contains dramatic and detailed descriptions of how Jeremiah felt about the situation in which he found himself:

> He has aged my flesh and my skin,
> And broken my bones.
> He has besieged me
> And surrounded me with bitterness and woe.
> He has set me in dark places
> Like the dead of long ago.
> He has hedged me in so that I cannot get out;
> He has made my chain heavy.
> Even when I cry and shout,
> He shuts out my prayer.
> He has blocked my ways with hewn stone;
> He has made my paths crooked. (verses 4-9)

> He has also broken my teeth with gravel,
> And covered me with ashes.
> You have moved my soul far from peace;
> I have forgotten prosperity.
> And I said, "My strength and my hope
> Have perished from the Lord."
> Remember my affliction and roaming,
> The wormwood and the gall.
> My soul still remembers
> And sinks within me. (verses 16-20)

And then he says in verse 21, "This I recall to my mind, therefore I have hope."

But wait—how did he get from the pessimism of verse 20 to the hope of verse 21? Something entered his mind as he wrote, something that gave him hope. And what he remembered is found in verses 22-23:

> Through the Lord's mercies we are not consumed,
> Because His compassions fail not.
> They are new every morning;
> Great is Your faithfulness.

Jeremiah remembered God's faithfulness and it gave him hope! It was from these verses that the hymn writer Thomas Chisholm took his inspiration for the hymn "Great Is Thy Faithfulness":

Great is Thy faithfulness, great is Thy faithfulness,
Morning by morning new mercies I see.

But what could Jeremiah see? He could see nothing with his eyes except a completely destroyed city and a devastated people. But he could see, with the eyes of faith, God's faithfulness. If the only time we declare the faithfulness of God is when we understand and see what He is doing, then we won't say it as often as we should. Many times in life we will see with our physical eyes only that which appears to confound our perception of who God is. But eyes of faith see not the circumstances but the faithfulness of God.

I once sat down next to a man on an airplane who pulled out a book to read titled *How We Die: Reflections on Life's Final Chapter*. He had buried two grandparents and his own mother, and suddenly he was looking for some answers about the end of life. I shared with him why I don't fear death but trust in the faithfulness of a loving God to see me across the gulf of death safely to heaven's shore.

Life is filled with challenges seen and unseen. Like Jeremiah, the only way we will be able to get through them is if we depend on the faithfulness of God. His faithfulness becomes a source of courage to all who trust in Him. We need to do what Jeremiah did: recall… remember… reckon… recollect… reprise the faithfulness of God and how He has delivered His people, including us, in the past.

Jim and Carol Cymbala started a church in the middle of Brooklyn, New York—and experienced numerous trials in the process. Their daughter experienced some deep difficulties, after which Carol was diagnosed with cancer. She told me how, during that time, she was on her face before God crying out, asking Him how He could have done all these things to them in light of their having given themselves to Him. What kind of reward was that? She said God spoke to her heart and said, "Carol, haven't I been faithful to you?" And from that experience she wrote a beautiful worship song where she says, "Looking back I can recall His mercy and His love."

You may not write a worship song that gets published, but your remembrance of God's faithfulness in your life will be good reason to have a new song in your heart.

Note

1. C. S. Lewis, *Reflections on the Psalms* (Orlando, FL: Houghton Mifflin Harcourt, 1958), 93-95.

PERSONAL QUESTIONS

1. In the Old Testament, the word "faithful" comes from the Hebrew root *aman*.

   a. Based on the overview, what does *aman* mean?

   b. Describe what it means to be faithful.

   c. What do we know for certain about the Lord in Deuteronomy 7:9?

2. Turn to the book of Psalms.

   a. In Psalm 50:15, what does God say He will do if we call upon Him?

   b. List the three promises God gives to those who call upon Him in Psalm 91:15.

      •

      •

      •

c. Do you feel that God hears you when you pray? Do you remember a time when you prayed and received an answer from God right away?

3. Read 2 Thessalonians 3:3.

a. From whom does the Lord guard us because He is faithful?

b. Is there a limit to the forgiveness and faithfulness of God?

c. We all have been overtaken by temptation at some point; but if we confess our sin, what will God faithfully do? (See 1 John 1:9.)

4. Read Lamentations 3:1-24. Note how Jeremiah goes from abject despair to a declaration of God's faithfulness. Write your own lament using this pattern. You may want to use a situation you've already gone through or one you're presently dealing with.

GROUP QUESTIONS

1. As a group, discuss the word "faithful" and how it comes from the Hebrew root *aman*.

   a. Discuss what the Hebrew word *aman* means.

   b. In your own words, describe what you think it means to be faithful.

   c. How does the Bible describe what it means to be faithful?

   d. What do we learn about the Lord in Deuteronomy 7:9?

2. Finish this sentence in the space below: Because God is faithful, we can…

   •

   •

   •

   •

3. Read Psalm 89:1-29 as a group. When we praise God for His faithfulness, we enjoy His faithfulness. We cement that truth deep within our soul, and it becomes the strength of our life.

   a. Name one way we can praise God for His faithfulness. (verse 1)

   b. Do you spontaneously praise God for His faithfulness? If not, what does that say about your enjoyment of Him?

   c. What instances of God's faithfulness does the psalmist mention in these verses?

   d. What are some ways we can continually praise God, no matter our circumstance?

4. Based on this lesson, what is your biggest takeaway about God's faithfulness? Share your answers with the group.

Lamentations is one of the most unique books in the Bible. It consists of 5 poems (funeral songs), each containing 22 verses (except the third which contains 66, or 22 x 3), composed around the time of Jerusalem's destruction in 586 B.C. The first four chapters use the literary device known as acrostic. Each line begins with the successive letter of the alphabet. In chapters 1 and 2, the first word of each verse begins with the successive 22 letters of the Hebrew alphabet (with slight variations in 2:16-17; 3:47-48; and 4:16-17). In chapter 3, all three lines of each stanza begin with the same (and successive) letter of the Hebrew alphabet. The fifth chapter is not an acrostic, but it does contain 22 verses, the same number of verses as letters in the Hebrew alphabet. It is a prayer rather than a lament over Jerusalem. In a time when there were few resources to produce additional copies, the acrostic format probably aided in memorization.

KNOWING
AN ETERNAL GOD

Psalm 90:2

*In this lesson we discover the
importance of eternity.*

OUTLINE

In a world controlled by clocks and calendars, where recorded years
number in the thousands, the idea of eternity seems somehow impractical.
Is eternity real, or just an idea? The Bible is unequivocal on the matter:
God dwells in eternity and has put eternity in the heart of every person.

  I.   **God Existed Before Time Began**

  II. **God Exists in the Past, Present, and Future
at the Same Moment**

 III. **God Exists Outside of Time**

 IV. **God Created Time**

  V. **God Controls Time**

For some people, the idea of eternity is right up near the top in the category of "Hardest-to-Believe Ideas in the Bible." I'm not sure why, given the incredible things that a lot of people believe today without a second thought (like evolution). But still, some people struggle with the idea that there is no beginning and there will be no end to God.

The Bible says that God is eternal, which means He exists endlessly. As far backward and forward as you can look, you see God. There was never a time when He was not, and never will be a time when He will cease. God is forever and ever; He is eternal. Connected to God's "always-ness" is His "everywhere-ness." Eternity means He has no beginning or end with regard to time, omnipresence means He has no limits as to space, and omniscience, no limits as to knowledge.

Many Bible verses speak of the eternity of God. In Isaiah 57:15, Isaiah refers to "the High and Lofty One who inhabits eternity." Eternity is like a house to God, a place where He dwells. Psalm 90:2 declares that "from everlasting to everlasting, You are God."

It's okay to struggle with comprehending the eternity of God (or any of His unlimited attributes). If we could understand Him fully, He would be no greater than ourselves. God has to be imponderable and incomprehensible to be God, doesn't He? We would be disappointed if we could unravel all the mysteries of God—there would be little room for faith. We have to go as far as our limited understanding will take us and then we hit a wall of non-understanding. When we get there, we drop to our knees and declare, "God, You are beyond finding out! You are greater than my understanding! What I understand about You, I worship; and what I can't understand I leave for You to teach me or not teach me in this life according to Your will. But in any case, I worship You as the eternal God."

Here's what we know about God's eternal nature.

GOD EXISTED BEFORE TIME BEGAN

Genesis 1:1 contains very familiar words to most people: "In the beginning God." Those four words summarize the doctrine of God's eternity. When "the beginning" began, God was there. Whenever that which has been created began, God was already there to create it.

One writer describes the difficulty in trying to comprehend God's eternity:

It is a concept that we, creatures of a physical world, cannot even begin to comprehend. It is like the blind trying to comprehend the sunset. Neither can we conceive of a world without time or space. We can speak of it, we can think of it, but the truth is that we cannot really imagine a phenomenon so foreign to our experience that anything is without that which dominates our lives every day, without time.

C. S. Lewis also had a helpful idea about how to compare time with eternity. If you could take hundreds of pieces of white paper, say 8.5 x 11 inches in size, and tape them all together to form a huge, white backdrop… then take that giant white "curtain" and tape it to the side of a large skyscraper… then take a pencil and go to the middle of that backdrop and make a small line about an eighth of an inch long—that line would represent time against the expanse of eternity. Time is a mere blip, a small mark, compared to eternity. (Of course, the illustration breaks down when you get to the edges of the white backdrop, as if eternity had limits. In reality, the white sheets go on forever.)

God is the white backdrop, and the span of history on earth is time. We exist against Him as the backdrop for everything.

GOD EXISTS IN THE PAST, PRESENT, AND FUTURE AT THE SAME MOMENT

One of the most amazing men I've ever known was a preacher named Andy. Once when Donna and I were visiting him in his home in Florida, he fascinated us with stories about great preachers whom I had only read about, but he had actually known. He had never been divorced, but was married to his third wife—the first two had died at much younger ages. At one point when he was telling us about something that happened, he stopped and turned to his wife and said, "Honey, did that happen with you or was that with Elizabeth?" Donna and I weren't sure whether to laugh or not, but then we all burst out laughing together. Because he had lived so long and been married to three wives, the events in each of the three marriages were hard to keep separate.

With us, events happen on a linear plane, one after the other. That's what we call history—the succession of events over time. But for God, there is no past, present, and future. He exists in all those "times" at once. He exists as much in this present moment as He does in the time of Abraham or in the time of the return of Christ. He sees and experiences all those events at once since He sees eternity all at once. "Then" is the same as "now" for God; "was" is the same as "is."

God's perspective on time can be illustrated this way: Say you attend the famous Rose Bowl Parade in Pasadena one year. You take a seat in the stands that are set up along the way and watch each beautiful float as it comes by, along with the horses, marching bands, and other participants. You see those events as they pass by in front of you, and you can even see them for a few moments after they've passed and before they arrive. But God sees the whole parade at once as if He were hovering in a helicopter high above all of history. Expand that idea beyond just the Rose Bowl Parade to include everything that is happening around the world and in the universe at that moment, and you have an idea of what it means for God to dwell in eternity.

Jesus confused and angered the Pharisees once by introducing the idea of His eternity into a discussion with them (John 8:48-59). He said, "Before Abraham was, I AM." I AM was the name by which God identified Himself to Moses in Exodus 3:14, the holy name of God. Jesus was saying that He existed before Abraham—that He was the great I AM of the Old Testament. The Pharisees thought Jesus was just a blasphemer pretending to be God; they didn't understand that He was, in fact, the eternal God.

When we are going through difficult times in our lives, we have to remember that God sees the present and the future at once. The present might be rife with difficulties, but the future contains the resolution of that situation which we can't see—but God can. Therefore, we must not give up in the present just because we can't see the future. We must trust that God is leading us toward a future that will work together for good even though we do not yet see what it is.

God Exists Outside of Time

This point is the obvious conclusion of the truth we just discussed. If God exists in the past, present, and future, then He obviously exists outside of time. Time is a temporary phenomenon, not an eternal one. When Adam and Eve sinned, everything changed. Life on earth became temporary instead of eternal as God put in motion a redemptive plan by which man's holiness might be restored and he might enter once again into eternal fellowship with God. Time as we know it—though it seems permanent—is only a temporary blip on the giant canvas of eternity. God stands outside of time (life on earth), looking down on it from His eternal perspective. It is very important for those of us who are bound by time to remember that God is not. Even though we are constrained by time at the present, our hearts still retain the call and longing for eternity (Ecclesiastes 3:11).

God Created Time

We know God created time on the basis of Genesis 1:14-19, the description of God putting the sun and moon in the heavens "to divide the day from the night; and… for signs and seasons, and for days and years"(verse 14). At that moment, God created time. And we live in the envelope called time.

God Controls Time

A Deist is someone who believes there is a God who created the world but who is not involved in running it. The example of a clockmaker is used to illustrate this idea of God: A clockmaker creates a clock, winds it up, and lets it run without further interference. God, the Deists say, created the world and its inhabitants and systems, and is now allowing it to run on its own without interference from Him. Many people try to explain why bad things happen to good people by saying God has taken a "hands-off" policy toward this world.

Deists are wrong. Their view has no biblical support whatsoever. God is definitely in control of the times and seasons of our lives. He knows the time of our birth, the events of our life, and the time of our death (Psalm 39:4-5; 139:13-16).

So what does the eternity of God mean to me in practical terms? It means something specific not just to Christians but to those who are seeking and those who do not believe as well.

First, the Christian and the eternity of God. Isaiah 40:28-31 provides wonderful reassurance for what it means to know the "everlasting God."

> Have you not known?
> Have you not heard?
> The everlasting God, the Lord,
> The Creator of the ends of the earth,
> Neither faints nor is weary.
> His understanding is unsearchable.
> He gives power to the weak,
> And to those who have no might He increases strength.
> Even the youths shall faint and be weary,
> And the young men shall utterly fall,
> But those who wait on the Lord
> Shall renew their strength;
> They shall mount up with wings like eagles,
> They shall run and not be weary,
> They shall walk and not faint.

The "everlasting God" is always there, and He is always with us. God is not bound by space or time or circumstance but is eternal and infinite.

Regardless of how your life may have come apart in the past or present, God sees it in the context of the future as well. He knows the future and what your life will be like! Couple that fact with His love and goodness (Jeremiah 29:11; Romans 8:28), and His eternity becomes a great reassurance. His strength is always there even though ours may leave us.

Second, the seeker and the eternity of God. If you are a person who is investigating Christianity, God, the Person of Jesus, or the reliability of the Bible, you are responding to that taste of eternity God has put in every human heart. Even though each of us is unique, we do share that common hunger to know and touch the eternal. Some have suggested that our hunger for eternity is what separates us from the rest of creation, what it means to be made in the image of God.

Because God is eternal, we who are created in His image have a longing to reconnect with the eternal. Every person created by God is going to live for eternity somewhere. Contrary to the naturalistic worldview present in our culture, we do not just die and contribute our carbon remains back to the dust. The human soul lives forever—the question is where.

There is hope in that fact (at least this life is not all there is), but here is also fear (not knowing where one is going to spend eternity). God looked upon the dual realities of man's mortality and God's immortality (eternity), and saw a conflict: "They were made to live with Me for eternity, but because they have been stained with sin, they can't."

To solve the dilemma, God the Father sent His only Son, Jesus Christ, into the world, the realm of mortality. In Christ, eternity touched time and a bridge for mankind into eternity was provided. By dying on a cross and providing cleansing from the stain of sin, Christ became the door through which mortal man can pass into immortality, to partake of the eternal life for which he has been longing. Putting one's faith in Christ is how we answer the question of where we will spend eternity. Embrace Christ and spend eternity with Him; reject Christ and spend eternity without Him.

Jesus said in John 5:24, "Most assuredly, I say to you, he who hears My word and believes in Him who sent Me has everlasting life, and shall not come into judgment, but has passed from death into life."

And John the apostle wrote in 1 John 5:11-13, "And this is the testimony: that God has given us eternal life, and this life is in His Son. He who has the Son has life; he who does not have the Son of God does not have life. These things I have written to you who believe in the name of the Son of God, that you may know that you have eternal life, and that you may continue to believe in the name of the Son of God."

Those are words of reassurance for the one who is seeking to touch eternity. It can only be accomplished by touching Christ.

Finally, the non-believer and the eternity of God. I hope you will ponder the words of Scripture I just quoted as an assurance to the seeker, for they apply to the one who will not believe as well. The Bible says there is a heaven for those who believe in Christ and a hell for those who don't. It is not a realm where you would want to live for a minute, much less an eternity.

God has put eternity in your heart, and you likely know it at this moment, regardless of your perspective toward Jesus Christ. May you choose, if you have not already done so, to spend eternity with Him. Eternal life is the gift He entered time to give.

1. Read Isaiah 57:15. The concept of eternity is something that is outside of our personal grasp.

   a. What does God inhabit?

   b. What can we conclude about God's existence since He created the heavens and earth in the beginning? (See Genesis 1:1.)

2. Read Genesis 1:14. We know God created time based on this verse.

   a. How did the creation of light cause a way to measure time?

   b. Do you think there was time before the creation of light?

   c. What can we determine about time in Revelation 22:5?

   d. What—or Who—will be the source of light in the New Jerusalem?

3. Read Isaiah 40:28-31.

   a. How does it make you feel to know that an eternal God knows you?

   b. What do those who wait on the Lord receive from the eternal God?

4. God is not bound by space or time. Instead, He is eternal and infinite.

   a. Read Jeremiah 29:11. What does God know because He is eternal?

   b. Should we fear the future? Why or why not?

   c. As Christ followers, what can be determined about our future? (Romans 8:28)

5. Read Ecclesiastes 3:11.

   a. What has God put in our heart?

   b. Why has He chosen to do this?

GROUP QUESTIONS

1. Read Isaiah 57:15 and Psalm 90:2 together.

   a. What does the Bible tell us about God in these verses?

   b. Why do you think the concept of eternity is hard for many people to grasp? Share your thoughts with the group.

2. How do we know that God existed before time began? (Genesis 1:1)

3. To an unsaved person questioning Christianity, how would you best explain the idea that God exists simultaneously—in the past, present, and future all at the same time?

4. Read Isaiah 40:28-31. What reassurance do these verses provide for believers?

5. Read John 5:24 as a group. What hope do we have because God sent His Son into the world?

6. Ecclesiastes 3:11 says, "He has put eternity in their hearts." As a group, take turns putting this verse into your own words.

   a. What do you think it will be like to be in a timeless environment one day? Can you catch an inkling of it? Why or why not?

   b. Why do you believe God put eternity in your heart? Have you already chosen to spend eternity with Him?

7. From this lesson, what have you learned about the importance of eternity? Discuss as a group.

DID YOU KNOW?

The Irish archbishop James Ussher (1581–1656) used scholarly methodology to determine how much time has passed since the creation. Using chronologies in the Old Testament (especially those in the early chapters of Genesis), multiple calendars based on different dating systems, and a reliable knowledge of the seasons, Ussher concluded that the world was created in 4004 B.C. According to Ussher's research, the age of our earth today is just over 6,000 years.

KNOWING A CHANGELESS GOD

Malachi 3:6

In this lesson we learn the ways God never changes.

OUTLINE

An old adage says, "The more things change, the more they stay the same." The point is, of course, that change is normal in human affairs. In fact, we get suspicious when things stay the same for too long. With God, the opposite is true. It is His unchanging nature that is the foundation of our faith.

I. **Because God Is Unchangeable, His Promises Are Unchangeable**

II. **Because God Is Unchangeable, His Purposes Are Unchangeable**

III. **Because God Is Unchangeable, His Provisions Are Unchangeable**

IV. **Because God Is Unchangeable, His Personality Is Unchangeable**

V. **Because God Is Unchangeable, His Prophecies Are Unchangeable**

The great London preacher Charles Spurgeon was driving through the countryside when he noticed a weather vane on top of a farmhouse. The windscreen on the weather vane had these words written on it: "God Is Love." Curious about such an unusual inscription for a weather vane, he stopped and knocked on the door of the farmhouse and inquired: "I just had to stop and ask about your weather vane. Do those words—'God Is Love'—mean that God's love changes as the weather changes?" The farmer replied, "Oh, no. What we mean is that whichever way the wind blows, God is still love."

Regardless of which way the wind blows, God's love never changes. And that applies to every other aspect of His nature as well. The unchangeableness of God's nature is referred to by theologians as His immutability. This means that all God has ever been, He will forever be; not only will He not change, He cannot change. God has no beginning and no end. He does not evolve and get wiser and wiser over the eons of time. God is often referred to as a rock in the Old Testament, referring to His stability and unchanging nature (2 Samuel 22:47).

Humans change in one of three ways, none of which apply to God. We either get better, we get worse, or we are moved by some influence or force acting upon us. None of those changes apply to God. For Him to change would mean that He got better or worse, which would deny the doctrine of His perfection. Because He is perfect, He cannot change or be moved.

We are living in an era in which change is occurring more rapidly than at any time in history. People are actually blaming their illness, in some cases, on not being able to cope with the rapidity of change happening around them. People are grasping for anything they can to try to stabilize themselves in our rapidly changing world. For those of us who know God, we don't need to grasp for anything else. God is more stable than the Rock of Gibraltar and Mount Everest combined. He is the Rock of our salvation, never changing and never moved.

A central passage of Scripture on the unchangeableness of God is Psalm 102:24-28:

> I said, "O my God,
> Do not take me away in the midst of my days;
> Your years are throughout all generations.
> Of old You laid the foundation of the earth,
> And the heavens are the work of Your hands.
> They will perish, but You will endure;
> Yes, they will all grow old like a garment;
> Like a cloak You will change them,

And they will be changed.
But You are the same,
And Your years will have no end.
The children of Your servants will continue,
And their descendants will be established before You."

Ironically, the Scripture is just as emphatic about the fact that Christians change dramatically as it is about the fact that God never changes. For instance, in 2 Corinthians 5:17 Paul wrote, "Therefore, if anyone is in Christ, he is a new creation; old things have passed away; behold, all things have become new." That's a definite change, is it not?

In addition to that fundamental change, there is incremental change as well: "But we all... are being transformed into the same image from glory to glory" (2 Corinthians 3:18). Beholding God daily in His Word changes us from the inside out "from glory to glory."

There is an ultimate, and final, change all Christians will experience when Christ returns for His own: "We shall not all sleep, but we shall all be changed" (1 Corinthians 15:51). When the Lord returns and summons us to Himself, we shall leave behind our mortality and be changed into immortality. We will be like Him as we see Him as He is (1 John 3:2).

We applaud those three changes: our changed nature, our incremental spiritual changes, and our ultimate transformation into beings fit for heaven. We are just as thankful that we *can* change as we are that God *can't*! In fact, we pray for change in our lives because we know how many areas there are which need to be conformed to Christ.

And yet there are many changes that we don't look forward to; some we even fear. We know there will be the inevitable loss of spouses and loved ones who leave us in a timely fashion, as well as those events and changes that occur in an untimely way—things we don't expect and wish would never happen. It is in the midst of those changes—the ones that bring heartache and perplexity—that we need to cling to the unchanging nature of God. Though our life may change, His never will. And if we remain anchored to Him, we will remain secure.

There are five reasons God's unchangeableness can make us secure in spite of the changes in our world.

BECAUSE GOD IS UNCHANGEABLE, HIS PROMISES ARE UNCHANGEABLE

Here is a key verse of Scripture on this point—Numbers 23:19:

God is not a man, that He should lie,
Nor a son of man, that He should repent.
Has He said, and will He not do?
Or has He spoken, and will He not make it good?

Growing up, did your family have a "Promise Box" on the kitchen or dining room table? The "Promise Box" held hundreds of the eight hundred promises of God in the Bible printed on little cards. At our house, someone would take out a card at each meal and read the promise of God that was on it. God's immutability means that not one of those promises—not one of the eight hundred—will ever be forgotten, violated, or unfulfilled. Why? Because what God says, He stands behind forever.

Here are some of the ones I remember reading as a child:

- God will never leave us nor forsake us (Hebrews 13:5).

- Jesus will come again and take us to Himself (John 14:3).

- Jesus will be with us even to the end of the age (Matthew 28:20).

Those favorites of mine, and your favorites, and all the rest of God's promises are as good today as the day they were spoken because God is unchangeable.

BECAUSE GOD IS UNCHANGEABLE, HIS PURPOSES ARE UNCHANGEABLE

Which do you think is more likely to stand the test of time—man's plan or God's purposes? We know the answer, and it's based on Proverbs 19:21: "There are many plans in a man's heart, nevertheless the Lord's counsel—that will stand."

For more documentation, Ezekiel 24:14 is strong: "I, the Lord, have spoken it; it shall come to pass." In the epic movie *The Ten Commandments*, Pharaoh often said, "So let it be written, so let it be done." But that's just a movie, and Pharaoh was just a man. But when God speaks something, it will indeed come to pass.

One of the most famous passages on the changeless purposes of God is Isaiah 46:9-11:

Remember the former things of old,
For I am God, and there is no other;
I am God, and there is none like Me,
Declaring the end from the beginning,
And from ancient times things that are not yet done,
Saying, "My counsel shall stand,
And I will do all My pleasure,"
Calling a bird of prey from the east,
The man who executes My counsel, from a far country.
Indeed I have spoken it;
I will also bring it to pass.
I have purposed it;
I will also do it.

Writing plans and mission and vision statements is in vogue today, and they are worthy disciplines. But as hard as we try, we cannot guarantee the outcome of what we plan. There is no end to the number of businesses that were hurt or ruined in March 2000, when the hi-tech sector of the stock market took a nosedive. Many were afraid it might happen, but no one knew when; so they kept on planning. On the heels of that event came the terrorist attacks of September 11, 2001, followed by the war in Iraq. Everyone's business plans and many people's individual plans (think of the thousands of reserve military people who were called from their work and homes to go to war) were dramatically changed. Plans and purposes are good, but no one can guarantee they will succeed.

Not only are God's plans perfect to begin with, they are always fulfilled. If you remember from the previous lesson, God's eternal nature means He sees the end of the plan at the same time He sees the beginning. It is all one completed picture from His perspective —the plan, the circumstances, the events, the disruptions, the human changes—they are all part of the plan.

There are some instances in Scripture where God appears to change His mind. Moses prayed, and God didn't judge Israel; Hezekiah prayed and didn't die; God didn't judge the Ninevites like He had planned; God said He was sorry He created mankind; God said He was sorry He had made Saul king. How do we explain these seeming changes in God's plans?

God communicates in human language. The Bible talks about God's arms, hands, and eyes, but then says He is a Spirit. The writers of the Bible used anthropomorphisms (assigning of human qualities to God) in order to communicate God's actions in terms we can easily understand. When human beings change their attitudes toward the purposes of God, and then God's purposes are carried out in response to man's responses, it appears that God changes His mind. But He doesn't, even though the Scripture describes it that way because it appears that way to us. In fact, God's purposes included the response of man. Though it may appear God's plan has changed, it has not.

BECAUSE GOD IS UNCHANGEABLE, HIS PROVISIONS ARE UNCHANGEABLE

Because God's provision flows from His unchanging promises, His provision is unchanging as well: "Every good gift and every perfect gift is from above, and comes down from the Father of lights, with whom there is no variation or shadow of turning" (James 1:17).

Who was the God who heard the prayers of Daniel in the lions' den; Shadrach, Meshach, and Abed-Nego in the fiery furnace; and Paul and Silas in the jail in Philippi? He is the same God you and I pray to when we are in our own perilous places. And because God is unchanging, His resources are as available to us as they were available to the saints of old. When I recall what God did for the heroes of the Bible, I have to remember that God lives in the "now" of our needs. At the same moment He saw and met Daniel's need, He sees and is ready to respond to our prayer for help as well. There is no "us" and "them" when it comes to God's provision—He is ready to meet our need at any time.

An old hymn, "Abide With Me," calls on the God who does not change to come in the hour of need. The first two verses say it well:

Abide with me. Fast falls the eventide.
The darkness deepens. Lord, with me abide.
When other helpers fail and comforts flee,
Help of the helpless, O abide with me.
Swift to its close ebbs out life's little day.
Earth's joys grow dim, its glories pass away.
Change and decay in all around I see.
Oh, Thou, who changest not, abide with me.

–H. F. Lyte

The One we need to abide with us is the One who changes not. What good would it do to call on someone whose character and nature changed with the situation or circumstance? The only reason we call on God with confidence is because we know that with Him there is no shadow of turning. All we have needed, His hand has provided. Great is His faithfulness! (From the hymn, "Great Is Thy Faithfulness"—T. O. Chisholm)

BECAUSE GOD IS UNCHANGEABLE, HIS PERSONALITY IS UNCHANGEABLE

I have to be careful as I introduce this section because of the risk of being misunderstood—but I believe every parent who reads this will understand completely! I've learned through the years that children know how to "work" their parents. Don't you agree? It's amazing how skilled they are at getting what they want. If they could apply that same creativity and energy to other things, the world would be a different place! Years ago, when I would collapse at the end of a typical Sunday—preaching, baptizing, receiving new Christians, receiving new members—my kids knew that was the time to hit me up for whatever they wanted—and they usually got it! Even when I knew they were coming after me, I seemed to be defenseless.

Well, I'm exaggerating a little bit, but only to make a point that is valid and to illustrate another point: We never, ever have to "work" our

Heavenly Father to get what we want. We don't have to wait until God is in a good mood, or wait until He's too tired to resist, or butter Him up with flattery. We don't have to accumulate "brownie points" by having our quiet time every day for a week, giving a large offering, or going to Sunday night and Wednesday night services.

God is always accessible to us, always in the same mood, always ready to hear from us, always ready to meet our needs. Hebrews 13:8 says it best: "Jesus Christ is the same yesterday, today, and forever." Isn't it a blessing to know that God's personality is as eternal and rock-solid as the rest of His nature?

BECAUSE GOD IS UNCHANGEABLE, HIS PROPHECIES ARE UNCHANGEABLE

To conclude, I would be unfaithful if I did not mention what will be, for some, a dark side of God's unchanging nature. Yes, it's true that God's promises, purposes, provisions, and personality are unchanging. But it is also true that His prophetic word about those who do not receive His promises and provision of salvation through Christ remains fully unchanged as well. The same God who says, "I am with you always" (Matthew 28:20), also says, "The soul who sins shall die" (Ezekiel 18:4, 20).

Dear reader, if you are waiting until the last minute of your life to consider accepting Christ, hoping God might change His mind about sin, or hoping you can talk Him into a different perspective, may I encourage you not to do so. God is as immutable and trustworthy in the hard things that He says as in the graceful. Since no one knows when the last moment of life will be (God knows), I urge you to receive the gift of His Son today and become an inheritor of His promises which will never change. Don't set yourself up for predictable heartache by hoping God will change. Instead, *you* change—and assure yourself that, whenever life's last moment comes, you will meet it with His eternal provision.

1. Read Psalm 102:24-28.

   a. What is the most important part of God's unchanging nature to you? Why?

   b. Does knowing that God never changes give you peace and reassurance? How so?

   c. Complete this sentence: Because God does not change, I...

2. Read Numbers 23:19.

   a. Because God is unchangeable, what can be determined about His promises?

   b. Which promises in the Bible are especially important to you?

   c. Reflect upon a time when God's promise(s) to you were fulfilled. What happened?

3. Go to the section titled, "Because God Is Unchangeable, His Purposes Are Unchangeable."

   a. Read Proverbs 19:21 and Ezekiel 24:14. According to these verses, what is more likely to stand the test of time—our plans or God's purposes?

   b. Why do you think God's plans are always perfect—in timing and fulfillment?

   c. Does it ever appear as if God changes His mind? If so, whose attitudes or actions is God responding to?

   d. We can see the changeless purposes of God in Isaiah 46:9-11. Think back on a time when you had to change your plans. What was the reason? Would God ever need to change plans because of that reason?

1. Read Psalm 102:24-28 together and discuss the unchangeable nature of God.

2. Read Numbers 23:19 as a group.

   a. Why are God's promises unchangeable?

   b. Discuss what you consider to be the most important part about God's unchanging nature. Why?

   c. Share if you had a "Promise Box" growing up. If so, what do you remember about it? Did it bring you comfort to know God's promises are true?

3. God's provisions are unchangeable. Our God is the same God that provided for Daniel and Paul.

   a. What encouragement do you find in knowing that the same God who provided for these people is the God you worship—and that He never changes?

   b. What does James 1:17 say about gifts from above? Is there any variation between the past and present?

   c. How has God provided for you? If comfortable, share with the group.

4. Do you ever feel like you need to put God in a good mood before you ask Him for something? Why do you think this is?

   a. Turn to Hebrews 13:8. What reassurance does this give you about Christ?

   b. Does knowing that God is unchanging change your viewpoint in dealing with Him? If so, in what ways?

DID YOU KNOW?

The term *anthropomorphism* comes from two Greek words: *anthropos* (man) and *morphe* (form). Therefore, an anthropomorphism is something that appears in the form of man, or human form. Human characteristics are assigned to God throughout the Bible, predominantly in the Old Testament. Reference is made to God's face (Psalm 34:16), eyes (2 Chronicles 16:9), mouth (Isaiah 1:20), ears (James 5:4), hands (Exodus 15:17), finger (Luke 11:20), arm (John 12:38), and foot (Lamentations 1:15). God is also said to have walked in the Garden of Eden (Genesis 3:8). The ultimate anthropomorphism occurred when God appeared on earth in the form of a human being, Jesus of Nazareth.

KNOWING A POWERFUL GOD

Revelation 19:6

In this lesson we are introduced to the power of God.

OUTLINE

In worldly terms, we are often reminded that "absolute power corrupts absolutely." That is, when humans acquire power, they often abuse it. That may be true with man, but not with God. He alone has absolute power and only uses it in a manner consistent with His righteous character.

I. **What the Bible Teaches About the Power of God**
    A. God Can Do All Things
    B. Nothing Is Too Hard for God
    C. God Never Gets Tired
    D. God Cannot Violate His Character

II. **How Can We Know God Is Powerful?**
    A. The Power of God Is Resident in Creation
    B. The Power of God Is Resident in Preservation
    C. The Power of God Is Resident in Resurrection

III. **Conclusion**
    A. This Truth Should Excite Us in Our Worship of God
    B. This Truth Should Encourage Us to Walk With God

Ayoung boy was standing around waiting to meet his family after church when the pastor happened by. Knowing this youth was a regular attendee in Sunday school, the pastor thought he would quiz the youngster to see what he had been learning. "Billy," the pastor began, "if you can tell me something God can do, I'll give you this apple." Without a moment's hesitation, Billy looked back at the pastor and said, "Pastor, if you can tell me something God can't do, I'll give you a whole box of apples!"

That young boy was the more astute theologian, wasn't he? He knew that God's power is unlimited, as Revelation 19:6 says: "Alleluia! For the Lord God Omnipotent reigns!" *Omnipotent* is a theological term for the great and awesome power of God. Literally, it means "all powerful." Fifty-eight times in the Bible we are told that God is almighty—the familiar "El Shaddai," in Old Testament terms. Daniel 4:35 puts it this way: "No one can restrain His hand or say to Him, 'What have You done?'"

The power of God in the Bible is not for power's sake but for the sake of carrying out His plans and purposes. Nothing can stand in His way.

WHAT THE BIBLE TEACHES ABOUT THE POWER OF GOD

As preliminary thoughts, here are four scriptural truths about the power of God.

God Can Do All Things

Nothing is any harder for God than anything else. This is a foreign concept to us since lifting one hundred pounds is definitely harder than lifting ten pounds. That's because our power and strength are limited. But since God's power is unlimited, nothing is too hard for Him. Job echoed this truth when he said to God, "I know that You can do everything, and that no purpose of Yours can be withheld from You" (Job 42:2).

Jesus echoed it as well in the context of saying that one thing (a rich man being saved) was harder than another thing (a camel going through the eye of a needle). In that comparative context, Jesus said that "with men it is impossible, but... with God all things are possible" (Mark 10:27).

Nothing Is Too Hard for God

In Genesis 18 we have a story that shows nothing is too hard for God: Abraham and Sarah had tried to have a child, but they remained childless. Then, when they were well past the childbearing age, God appeared to Abraham and told him Sarah would give birth to a son.

Sarah heard God make this promise and laughed out loud. And God asked, "Is anything too hard for the Lord?" (verse 14)

We probably would have laughed like Sarah did. When the baby was born, he was named Isaac, which means "laughter." From then on, Abraham and Sarah probably laughed to themselves at the power of God that was able to break the rules of nature and give them a child in their old age.

God Never Gets Tired

The Old Testament prophet Isaiah made this declaration about God: "The everlasting God, the Lord, the Creator of the ends of the earth, neither faints nor is weary" (Isaiah 40:28).

I remember undergoing physical therapy once to strengthen the muscles in my legs—when I left those sessions, my legs were on fire. All during the sessions, the therapist would say, "Are you tired yet?" And, of course, I would say "No," even though I was dying. When I think about the fact that God could do all those repetitions of exercises without ever tiring—He could do them for eternity without even stopping—I am amazed. But the Word of God says that He never faints (weakens) or gets weary. He never has less power, say, after leading the Israelites through a mighty military campaign, than He does "first thing in the morning." All of the ways we are used to thinking about strength go out the window when thinking of God.

God Cannot Violate His Character

When I was in seminary, all of us young, we would carry on deep discussions around the table in the lunch area. We entertained such profound questions as, "How many angels can dance on the head of a pin?" Another question that came up occasionally was, "Can God create a rock so big that He can't pick it up?" If the answer is no, He's not powerful enough to create such a huge rock; if yes, He's not powerful enough to pick it up. Either way, His power is limited.

The fault in this question is that it doesn't have to do with God's power but with God's character. And the exercise of God's power is always governed by the constraints of His character. Three things about His character are important.

1. God Cannot Lie

   The Bible says that God "cannot lie" (Titus 1:2). It doesn't say He would not lie but that He cannot lie. There is in God no darkness at all, which means that He cannot lie (1 John 1:5). If God ever lied about one little thing, His entire character would implode; He would no longer be trustworthy in any matter.

2. God Cannot Deny Himself

In addition to not being able to lie, God cannot deny Himself: "If we are faithless, He remains faithful; He cannot deny Himself" (2 Timothy 2:13). This means He cannot be, nor will be, anything that is contrary to His own perfection.

3. God Cannot Be Tempted or Tempt Anyone

James 1:13 says, "God cannot be tempted by evil, nor does He Himself tempt anyone." This is a good point by which to evaluate the question about the rock and God's power. Satan tempted Jesus to do certain things solely for the purpose of demonstrating His power, and Jesus refused because it was not consistent with His character (Matthew 4:1-11). Just so, God would never enter into a test such as creating a rock too big to pick up. That is an interesting philosophical speculation, but not a legitimate or serious question to raise regarding a holy, perfect God. Why? Because, simply put, God is not a show-off. It's not consistent with His character.

Sometimes we wonder why God doesn't exercise His power on our behalf. The answer is that God only exercises His power in accordance with His purposes. Perhaps you can think now, in hindsight, of a prayer you prayed that God didn't answer "Yes" to, that you are glad He didn't. God doesn't exercise His power at times because He can see the future and knows what's best.

How Can We Know God Is Powerful?

What evidence would you set forth from the Scriptures to demonstrate that God is powerful? Here are three dominant categories by which we know that God is powerful.

The Power of God Is Resident in Creation

One of the most prominent verses dealing with God's power is Romans 1:20: "For since the creation of the world His invisible attributes are clearly seen, being understood by the things that are made, even His eternal power and Godhead, so that they are without excuse." With powerful telescopes and space probes, we are learning more and more about our universe. It is bigger and more complex than we ever imagined. And Paul, even with his limited knowledge, says that what is visible with the naked eye is enough to convince an observant person that a powerful God exists.

Then there are the creation passages in Genesis. Time after time in Genesis 1 the text reads, "Then God said... and it was so." God didn't fashion the earth with His hands, He simply spoke it into existence out of nothing (Genesis 1; Psalm 33:6, 9). When Job was arguing (foolishly) with God, God asked him, "Where were you when I laid the foundations of the earth?" (Job 38:4) Shortly after that, Job laid his hand over his mouth—he had no answer for God (Job 40:4).

One writer, commenting on the attribute of God's power, pointed out that the same God who created a ring one hundred thousand miles in diameter around Saturn created a tiny colored feather in the wing of a hummingbird. His power and perfection are as evident in the largest parts of creation as they are in the smallest.

The Power of God Is Resident in Preservation

What if God had created the world and then withdrawn, allowing it to be preserved (or not preserved) by itself? The same power of God that created the world keeps the world together. Everything is upheld "by the word of His power" (Hebrews 1:3).

Jeremiah 10:13 gives testimony to the ongoing activity of God in His creation:

When He utters His voice,
There is a multitude of waters in the heavens:
"And He causes the vapors to ascend from the ends of the earth.
He makes lightning for the rain,
He brings the wind out of His treasuries."

Let me encourage you also to turn to Psalm 104 and read verses 5-30, one of the most beautiful passages in the Bible on God's creation. Perhaps the first and last verses of this lengthy section summarize the whole: "You who laid the foundations of the earth, so that it should not be moved forever.... You send forth Your Spirit, they are created; and You renew the face of the earth" (Psalm 104:5, 30).

What do you think would happen if, for one moment, Almighty God withdrew His sustaining and renewing hand from this universe? It would fly off into oblivion and chaos. The same God who created all things is also the God who holds them together. Jesus Christ "is before all things, and in Him all things consist" (Colossians 1:17).

The Power of God Is Resident in Resurrection

There is no doubt among theologians, and probably laymen as well, that the most powerful demonstration of God's power is the resurrection of Jesus Christ. In Ephesians 1, Paul says that the same power that was at work to choose and save us is the power "which He worked in Christ when He raised Him from the dead and seated Him at His right hand in the heavenly places" (Ephesians 1:20).

If you could choose to know any kind of power in the world, what would it be? Would it be the power of an earthquake? A volcano? The power God exercised to create the universe? As mighty as those are, there is an even greater power, which Paul said he desired to know: "That I may know [Christ] and the power of His resurrection" (Philippians 3:10). To know the power of Christ's resurrection would be to know the supreme power of God.

CONCLUSION

So much more could be said about the power of God, which space will not allow. But let me conclude this lesson by noting two ways the power of God should impact our lives.

This Truth Should Excite Us in Our Worship of God

Pascal once wrote that the greatest single distinguishing feature of the omnipotence of God is that our imagination gets lost when we try to think of it. Isn't that true? We feel utterly inadequate to try to comprehend the power of God and what it has done and can accomplish.

When the Christian comes to something he cannot comprehend, his response should be to fall down before God in worship. The incomprehensibility of God cannot be addressed at the human level. We have to take by faith what is revealed of Him in Scripture and verified by His acts in history, and then worship Him for that part of Him which is told to us but which we simply cannot comprehend. We do not have to comprehend everything about God in order to worship Him.

Moses led the children of Israel in a mighty song of worship and praise after seeing God part the Red Sea and destroy Pharaoh's armies (Exodus 15). Verse 11 of that song says, "Who is like You, O Lord, among the gods? Who is like You, glorious in holiness, fearful in praises, doing wonders?"

I hope you have experienced God doing things in your life more powerful than you can understand, and have fallen to your knees in worshipful response.

This Truth Should Encourage Us to Walk With God

Our link to the power of God is this: The same power that raised Jesus from the dead is at work in us. Paul says in 1 Corinthians 6:14 that "by his power God has raised the Lord from the dead and will also raise us from the dead" (NCV). We have been raised from the dead spiritually by God's power, and will be raised from the dead literally one day when Christ returns to receive unto Himself those who are His.

Sadly, not many Christians live their lives in the power of God. I think most Christians live in the power of their own human flesh the majority of the time. They live that way until they run into some sort of crisis—a power outage, if you will. A power outage in the spiritual life is like going to the doctor and discovering that something has shown up in your test results that he wasn't expecting and for which he doesn't have a simple cure. It's like going to work one day at the same place you've worked for 25 years and being given a pink slip saying your services are no longer needed. It's like getting a call at 1:00 in the morning telling you your child has been killed in a car accident at college. A power outage is any of the infinite number of events in life which we are not prepared to handle.

Most of us don't touch the power of God until we are overwhelmed with our own weakness. And then we discover that when we are weak, He is strong (2 Corinthians 12:9-10). It is then that we discover we can "do all things through Christ who strengthens me" (Philippians 4:13).

A. B. Simpson was the founder of one of the great missionary agencies of a previous generation. He was a godly and spiritually powerful man. I have read and profited from many of his writings. A. B. Simpson went through his own power outage in his mid-forties. He just burned out—lost his health, his ministry, and was defeated and discouraged. Then one day he heard the words of an old spiritual—"Nothing is too hard for Jesus, no man can work like Him"—and it hit him: He had been trying to do the work of God in his own strength. As a result, he rededicated himself to the work of God and never had another power outage in his life.

I encourage you to be excited and encouraged by the power of God in your own life. May your worship and your walk reflect the reality of His power at work in you.

PERSONAL QUESTIONS

1. Read Revelation 19:6.

   a. What does the term *omnipotent* mean?

   b. Can anything stand in God's way?

   c. What does Jesus say in Mark 10:27?

2. Read the story of Abraham and Sarah's child of promise in Genesis 18:1-15.

   a. What was Sarah's response when the Lord said she would have a son? (verse 12)

   b. Has God ever promised you something you laughed or scoffed at? If so, what was it?

   c. How does the Lord respond in situations like this? (verse 14)

d. Do you ever feel that you hold yourself back from the possibilities of God's power?

3. Read James 1:12-17. Have you ever heard anyone blame God for not stopping them from doing something wrong?

   a. Who is responsible for temptation?

   b. God's power is in keeping with His character. What main attribute of God would keep Him from lying or tempting?

4. Look at Jeremiah 10:13 in the section titled, "The Power of God Is Resident in Preservation."

   a. What do you think would happen if God had created the world and then left it to survive on its own?

   b. What are we assured of through the word of God's power? (Hebrews 1:3)

1. Read Revelation 19:6 together.

   a. How would you describe God's absolute power?

   b. What does the theological term *omnipotent* mean?

   c. Why can nothing stand in God's way? How come God can do anything? (Mark 10:27)

2. Read Genesis 18:1-15 as a group.

   a. What was God able to accomplish for Abraham and Sarah?

   b. What was Sarah's reaction? (verse 12)

   c. What was God's response? (verse 14)

   d. Has there been a time when you laughed at God when He promised you something? If comfortable, share with the group what happened.

3. Isaiah 40:28 says God "neither faints nor is weary."

   a. How does this verse give you comfort in His power?

   b. Does knowing that God never loses His power give you strength? How so?

4. Based on this lesson, how can we know that God is powerful? Fill in the blanks below.

   a. The power of God is _____.

   b. The power of God is _____.

   c. The power of God is _____.

   d. If speaking to a non-Christian, what evidence would you present from Scripture that demonstrates God's power? Discuss as a group.

5. Read 2 Corinthians 12:9-10.

   a. What lesson can we learn from this passage?

   b. Share with the group how this passage encourages you in your life.

Power and authority are closely related ideas; they are similar, but separate (Luke 4:36). Authority (*exousia*) has more to do with the right to exercise power, while power (*dunamis;* cf. dynamite) is the actual force or strength necessary to get things done. God is pictured in the Bible as the source of all authority (Daniel 2:21; 7:13-14). Any authority exercised by others is authority given to them by God—for example, civil authorities on earth (Romans 13:1). Any exercise of power lacking such delegated authority is illegitimate and will be punished by God. For example, in the Old Testament, the abuses of authority by the priest Eli's sons (1 Samuel 1–4), by King Saul (1 Samuel 15), and by the sons of the high priest, Aaron (Leviticus 10). Authority can be conveyed by God to men, and with it appropriate power, as Jesus did with His disciples (Matthew 10:1). Though Satan has some authority at present (1 John 5:19), his authority is subject to God's. Christians are transferred from the authority of darkness to the Kingdom of God at the time of their conversion (Colossians 1:13).

KNOWING
A GOOD GOD

Psalm 52:1

In this lesson we learn the ways God demonstrates His goodness.

OUTLINE

Christians are committed to keeping the way of salvation focused on faith, not being good or bad—and rightly so. But goodness is good! The greatest example we have of how to be good is God Himself. Like all His attributes, goodness is an essential part of His character.

I. **God's Goodness Is Seen in His Provision for All of Our Needs**

II. **God's Goodness Is Seen in His Patience With Us**

III. **God's Goodness Is Seen in the Way He Protects Us**

IV. **God's Goodness Is Seen in the Path He Chooses for Us**

Lewis Smedes' book *A Pretty Good Person* takes an interesting slant on the concept of goodness in people. A pretty good person, he says, has a little gratitude, a little grit, some basic integrity, an eye for what's going on around him, and a willingness to love fairly. In other words, he defines goodness relatively—a pretty good person is a better-than-average person. While he doesn't offer his definition as a standard, he accomplishes his goal of encouraging his readers to be better people. It's hard to disagree with that goal. Who could argue with the idea of having more good people in the world?

But his thesis stops at the line that separates man from God. God is not "better-than-average"; His goodness is not measured on a relative scale. God's goodness is, like His other attributes, absolute and pure. When we read a statement like Nahum 1:7, "The Lord is good," we are reading a grammatical statement that equates God with goodness. (See "God is love" in 1 John 4:8, 16.)

Psalm 52:1 says that "the goodness of God endures continually," meaning it is never absent from God's character. Goodness is ever-present with God.

We can connect God's goodness with His grace, His mercy, His perfection—almost all of His attributes can be thought of as expressions of His goodness. But the one characteristic that comes to mind more than any other when I think of God's goodness is His generosity. That means God is good abundantly. His goodness overflows in its extravagance.

More than twenty years ago, I heard Lloyd Ogilvie, retired chaplain of the United States Senate, preach at a Bible conference in Ocean City, New Jersey. His message was on the story of the prodigal son in Luke 15. About halfway through his preaching on this familiar passage, he stopped and said, "By the way, I have given you the wrong title for my message. The correct title is 'The Prodigal Father.'" He explained how the word *prodigal* meant lavish, unrestrained, uninhibited, and almost wasteful. It is usually applied to the son who left home and spent his inheritance in unrestrained, wasteful living. But it really should be applied, he said, to the father who, when the son returned home, lavished love on the son in an unrestrained, uninhibited, generous-to-a-fault way. He was a prodigal father, prodigal in the way he lavished love so generously on his prodigal son.

That's the way God is. He lavishes goodness on us, His children, in totally unrestrained ways. He is generously good toward us.

God's Goodness Is Seen in His Provision for All of Our Needs

Psalm 145 is a classic passage on the goodness of God seen in His provisions for our needs. Verses 6-7 say,

Men shall speak of the might of Your awesome acts,
And I will declare Your greatness.
They shall utter the memory of Your great goodness,
And shall sing of Your righteousness.

And verses 14-16 declare,

The Lord upholds all who fall,
And raises up all who are bowed down.
The eyes of all look expectantly to You,
And You give them their food in due season.
You open Your hand
And satisfy the desire of every living thing.

Psalm 136:25 says that God "gives food to all flesh, for His mercy endures forever." And Psalm 33:5 speaks summarily by saying, "The earth is full of the goodness of the Lord." Think about the abundantly generous way in which God has exercised His goodness toward us in the earth. He could have provided a manna-like substance to meet our nutritional needs. Instead, He filled the earth with a variety of foods that are a delight to behold as well as to consume. God's creativity in meeting our needs is a hallmark of His generosity.

Think of the creation itself. It could have been fashioned so as to be consistent from one coast to the other or from one continent to another. But instead, there is a great variety in the handiwork and provision of God. We can actually choose the kind of geography in which we would like to live, so abundant are the different environments. It is a shame that we don't take the opportunity to fulfill the words of Psalm 34:8: "Oh, taste and see that the Lord is good." Many of us live in or near areas of absolute beauty and grandeur that we rarely sample. We would get an incredible taste of the goodness of God in creation if we would move a little beyond our daily routines and sample what God has provided. The flowers, the scenery, the animal life, the acres of crops growing and waving in the wind—the evidence of God's goodness is everywhere we turn.

God's Goodness Is Seen in His Patience With Us

God's patience is mentioned in the context of His goodness probably more than any other attribute. The Psalms look at the patience of God in terms of His mercy. Grace is getting something we don't deserve, and mercy is not getting something we do deserve. If we are not judged for our sins (judgment being what we deserve), it is because of God's mercy.

Psalm 107:1 says, "Oh, give thanks to the Lord, for He is good! For His mercy endures forever." And Psalm 100:5 says, "His mercy is everlasting." So God is patient with us in that He does not give us what we deserve. Every person alive in this world should be praising and thanking God daily for His mercy. When I hear Christians talking about getting what is "rightfully theirs," I am reminded of how thankful I am that God doesn't give us what is rightfully ours.

Psalm 107:8-9 contains a refrain that is echoed throughout the psalm about the goodness of God:

Oh, that men would give thanks to the Lord for His goodness,
And for His wonderful works to the children of men!
For He satisfies the longing soul,
And fills the hungry soul with goodness.

The phrase, "Oh, that men would give thanks to the Lord for His goodness, and for His wonderful works to the children of men," is repeated in verses 15, 21, and 31. Over and over in this psalm is the message that God has dealt with us according to mercy. If you and I had been God, as far back as the Garden of Eden, we would not have been nearly so patient with our own sins as God has been. But God forgave us generously. He didn't forgive with restriction on our happiness; He forgave and gives us joy and freedom as if we had never sinned at all. We enjoy great extravagance and blessing from the hand of God, and yet still find time and reason to complain about His treatment of us.

I declare to you without hesitation or reservation that God is good. He provides for us, gives us every good thing we need, and is patient with us when we fail. We have no right to expect anything more than what God has given us.

Some people wonder why God blesses everyone—the good and bad alike. Here's a simple way to remember how God dispenses His goodness: He gives some of His goodness to all the people, and all of His goodness to some of the people, while none of the people deserve any of His goodness. You will live a life angry at God because you don't think you're getting what you deserve out of life if you don't remember God's mercy—that you are not getting what you actually deserve. God really is a good God.

God's Goodness Is Seen in the Way He Protects Us

To get ordained into the Christian ministry is (usually) a rigorous ordeal. You have to write a long paper covering all your theological beliefs. Then a panel of pastors and seminary professors comes together on a given day to listen to you present your paper, after which they try to poke holes in it by asking you all kinds of difficult doctrinal questions. I'm glad it's something you do only once!

During my ordination exam, while being asked about my views on angels, one of the panel members asked, "Mr. Jeremiah, there is no statement in your paper about guardian angels. Do you believe in the doctrine of guardian angels?" Both my father, who was a college president and a pastor, and my mother were attending the examination, and when I was asked that question my mother said, "I don't know if he does, but I do." Just like that—right out in the middle of the examination. I don't know if she meant to say it or if it just popped out of her mouth. What she was expressing was the fact that there had been many times when God's grace kept me from becoming just a memory to my dear mother.

Once when I was about nine or ten years of age, I was staying with my uncle for a few days on his dairy farm in Pennsylvania. He had two large, very tall silos on his farm where silage for the cows was stored. The silos had ladder-like steps going up the outside to a small door allowing you to enter the silo from the top, so I decided to climb up and jump down onto the silage and play inside the silo. After climbing all the way to the top, I opened the small door and was just about to jump when I noticed the silo was empty. I knew one of the two silos was full of silage, but I had picked the wrong one. I came within inches of jumping out into thin air and probably losing my life or being severely injured by the fall. It was years of things like that which prompted my mother to answer out loud.

Each of us has had some similar circumstance in life where we have been protected from harm by God's grace. The psalmist David apparently had the same thought when he wrote, "I would have lost heart, unless I had believed that I would see the goodness of the Lord in the land of the living" (Psalm 27:13). The whole psalm is about God's protection from fear and enemies and the dangers of war. In the opening verse he wrote, "The Lord is my light and my salvation; whom shall I fear? The Lord is the strength of my life; of whom shall I be afraid?"

Anyone who doesn't believe in the protective goodness of God does not believe because they don't know what they don't know. If we could see behind the scenes all the times when God has protected us from harm, we would think differently. The children of Israel complained loudly when Moses led them through the wilderness of Sinai to get to the Promised Land. What they didn't know was that God had spared them from a crushing defeat at the hands of the Philistines by taking the route they did (Exodus 13:17-18).

The next time you're stuck in traffic or take a wrong turn, before you complain, stop and remember God's goodness. Your delay might be just an experience in patience-building, or it might have been God's way of protecting you from something far worse.

God's Goodness Is Seen in the Path He Chooses for Us

Sometimes we get the mistaken idea that if God were really good, He wouldn't shackle us with restrictions and limitations on our lives. For example, we read in Matthew 7:13-14, "Enter by the narrow gate; for wide is the gate and broad is the way that leads to destruction, and there are many who go in by it. Because narrow is the gate and difficult is the way which leads to life, and there are few who find it."

Rather than being a limitation on our lives, the path God has chosen for our lives is a demonstration of His goodness toward us. There are four sets of contrasts in Matthew 7:13-14: two gates (wide and narrow), two ways (broad and difficult), two groups of people (many on one road and few on the other), and two destinations (destruction and life). If you were a non-Christian looking at the two options ahead of you, which would you choose? No doubt you would choose the broad way and the wide gate, right?

It's the last of the four sets of contrasts that puts the choices in perspective. If you're going through the wide gate on the broad way surrounded by a huge crowd of people, you think you're doing the right thing until you realize that the way you're on leads to destruction. And if you choose the narrow gate on the difficult way and you look around and there aren't many people with you, you are going to think you made a serious mistake—until you realize the difficult way leads to life.

In preaching on this passage, one pastor called his message "Narrow Gate Theology." He says it sounds discriminating, politically incorrect, and un-American to talk about taking the minority view. Don't we believe in "majority rule"? We can thank God that Jesus did not fall into the "majority rule" trap. He would never have made it to the Cross if He had taken the broad way and wide gate along with the crowds in Jerusalem.

The broad way is a lifestyle unencumbered by moral guidelines and restrictions. There are no moral stop signs or speed limits to slow you down in your pursuit of pleasure and fulfillment in this life. You're free to pick and choose from whatever makes you feel good along life's way. You feel wild and free and immortal and invincible.

The narrow way is the difficult way where we are exhorted to "get a life," "live a little," and "color outside the lines once in a while." We are viewed as backward and weird and repressive. We are husbands and wives who stay together for better or for worse, parents who commit themselves to their children instead of chasing the dollar, and families who spend time in church and the community trying to make a difference. The narrow road, to the folks on the broad road, doesn't look like much of a way to live. But it's the only way to live if life, not destruction, is your goal.

Those on the narrow way are like children who, having grown up into successful and fulfilled adults, look back and thank God they had parents who established boundaries for their lives. Out of His heart of goodness, God has put boundaries along the narrow road to make sure those on it reach their destination: life eternal.

God's provision, patience, protection, and path are all evidences of God's goodness manifested in His love for you. If you haven't recently, take a moment to thank God for being so good.

1. God's goodness is absolute. What distinguishable characteristic of His goodness can we see in Nahum 1:7? What about in Psalm 52:1?

2. Read Psalm 34:8.

   a. What do you think "taste and see that the Lord is good" means in regard to His creation?

   b. What beautiful and natural things is the region where you live known for?

   c. Describe the beauty of a waterfall, a river, a lake, or an ocean that you've seen. Have you ever felt God's goodness in the presence of His creation?

   d. Why do you think God made our world so beautiful?

3. Read Psalm 107:1 and 100:5. The goodness of God is often associated with His patience and mercy.

   a. What do you personally know of the mercy of God?

   b. When those who follow Christ fail, they are not judged for their sins because God is patient and merciful. What do these verses say about His mercy?

4. Have you ever been saved from harm and realized you must have been protected by God? If so, what was the occasion?

5. In Psalm 27:1 and 13, David knew the Lord would protect him from harm. Why didn't he lose heart?

GROUP QUESTIONS

1. Based on this lesson, in what ways is God's goodness seen? Discuss as a group.

   a. What do Nahum 1:7 and Psalm 52:1 say about His goodness?

   b. What can we connect God's goodness to? Specifically, which of His attributes?

2. Turn to the section titled, "God's Goodness Is Seen in His Provision for All of Our Needs." Then read Psalm 145:6-7, 14-16 together.

   a. In what way does God provide for our needs?

   b. What will men speak of? (verse 6)

   c. Whom does the Lord raise up? (verse 14)

3. Read Matthew 7:13-14 as a group.

   a. Name one aspect of the narrow gate which is difficult for you.

   b. What would most likely be the result if you took the broad way in this issue?

   c. What would be the result if you took the difficult way?

d. Think of some people you know who have taken the broad way. What is their life like in comparison with the people who chose the narrow gate?

e. What can you do to stay focused and follow the path God has chosen for you?

f. Do you believe part of God's goodness can be seen in that path?

DID YOU KNOW?

The Golden Rule—"Whatever you want men to do to you, do also to them, for this is the Law and the Prophets" (Matthew 7:12)—is the classic standard for exercising goodness at the human level. Interestingly, the Golden Rule did not originate with Jesus. History noted that, around 20 A.D., the Jewish Rabbi Hillel was challenged by a Gentile to summarize the Jewish law in the short time that the Gentile could stand on one leg. Hillel reportedly responded, "What is hateful to you, do not do to anyone else. This is the whole law; all the rest is commentary. Go and learn it." While Hillel phrased the rule negatively, Jesus turned it around and phrased it positively as a proactive rule; an exhortation for being good to others in the way you would want others to be good to you. Statements similar to the Golden Rule also appear in Hinduism, Buddhism, and Confucianism.

KNOWING AN ALL-KNOWING GOD

Psalm 139:2-4

*In this lesson we learn what it means that
God knows everything.*

OUTLINE

Beginning in the Garden of Eden, God made it clear that He knows everything about those created in His image. This can be a comfort— He knows and understands our pain—and a cause for concern—He knows all our sins. Our greatest challenge is to live in the light of His omniscience.

I.   **God's Omniscience and Our Prayers**

II. **God's Omniscience and Our Suffering**

III. **God's Omniscience and Our Fellowship With Him**

IV. **God's Omniscience and Our Sin**

OVERVIEW

Most people go their whole lives without experiencing something you would think would be normal: a relationship with at least one person who knows them completely. Everyone would like to know that there is at least one person to whom they could reveal anything without the fear of being judged or rejected. People live their whole lives without being able to talk about their deepest fears, longings, hurts, or dreams.

While it's true that relationships on this earth don't always reach the stage of intimacy they should, that doesn't mean there is no one who knows you completely. We forget that God knows everything about us and extends an invitation to us to know and be known in His presence. Psalm 139 is the classic text in the Bible on the "all-knowingness" of God—what theologians call His omniscience. The first four verses of this psalm present some startling truths about how God knows us:

Verse 1: A summary statement—God knows us.

Verse 2: He knows all our activities, all the routines of our life, and our thoughts (Ezekiel 11:5).

Verse 3: God knows our directions, our ways, and our habits.

Verse 4: He knows every word we speak.

And verse 16 says that God knows all the days of our lives. That is a level of detail that no one else knows about you.

The rest of the Bible confirms God's all-knowing nature:

- 1 John 3:20: God knows everything.
- Acts 15:18: God knows everything He has done and created.
- Job 37:16: God's knowledge is perfect, lacking nothing.
- Isaiah 46:9-10: God knows everything from eternity past to eternity future.
- Psalm 33:13-15: Nothing escapes God's vision from His vantage point in heaven.
- Psalm 147:4: God knows all the stars by name.
- Matthew 10:29-30: God knows the condition of every sparrow and knows the number of hairs on our head.
- Job 38–41: God knows every detail about the natural world.

Think of what God's knowledge is like compared to ours. Because He knows all things perfectly, He doesn't know one person better than another. He doesn't learn or discover; His knowledge is complete at all times. God is never surprised or amazed; He doesn't wonder about anything since He knows everything. God's knowledge never fades or grows dim or retreats into the recesses of His memory or subconscious. He knows every possible item of knowledge concerning everything that has ever existed or will exist in the future. God doesn't have to count anything (the grains of sand on the seashore, the stars in the sky, the flowers in a given field)—all knowledge in the universe is ever-present in His mind.

Everything I just stated about God's knowledge is the opposite of how it is with us. Our knowledge is imperfect and limited, His is perfect and complete. In fact, not only does God know everything that is actual, He even knows everything possible. Once, when addressing the residents of two towns called Chorazin and Bethsaida, Jesus said, "Woe to you, Chorazin! Woe to you, Bethsaida! For if the mighty works which were done in you had been done in Tyre and Sidon, they would have repented long ago in sackcloth and ashes" (Matthew 11:21). How could anyone possibly know what might have happened under a certain set of circumstances if they had indeed come to pass? In fact, in our court system, if an attorney asks a "What if…?" question to a witness, the witness's attorney will immediately object: "Calls for speculation!" And the objection will normally be sustained. Why? Because we can't possibly know what might happen under any given set of ircumstances.

But God knows! He knows everything that has happened and everything that might have happened. We cannot even comprehend that kind of knowledge, of course. But that's the whole point: God is God, and we're not. No wonder David wrote in Psalm 139:6, "Such knowledge is too wonderful for me; it is high, I cannot attain it."

Here is how God's omniscience impacts four areas of our spiritual life.

GOD'S OMNISCIENCE AND OUR PRAYERS

Jesus' teaching on prayer in Matthew 6:5-8 is a place where God's omniscience intersects with the practical matter of prayer.

> And when you pray, you shall not be like the hypocrites. For they love to pray standing in the synagogues and on the corners of the streets, that they may be seen by men. Assuredly, I say to you, they have their reward. But you, when you pray, go into your room, and when you have shut your door, pray to your Father who is in the secret place; and your Father who sees in secret will reward you openly. And when you pray, do not use vain repetitions as the heathen do. For they think that they will be heard for their many words. Therefore do not be like them. For your Father knows the things you have need of before you ask Him.

We are not to act like the heathen who think they have to help God hear their prayers by praying long, repetitive prayers. We do not pray to inform God—He already knows what we need before we ask Him. We pray in order to fellowship with Him and discern His will. We, not God, are changed by our prayers. Even with regard to our daily needs, Jesus says, "Your heavenly Father knows that you need all these things" (Matthew 6:32).

The fact that God already knows our needs immediately raises the question, "Why, then, pray at all?" More than any other reason, we pray out of obedience—God has commanded us to pray.

But there are other reasons as well. Sometimes we think we know what we need, but our Heavenly Father knows what we really need. Sometimes He changes our heart about what we're asking for while we're praying. Since God knows all things actual and possible, it is a comfort to know that He can tell us what we need instead of us having to tell Him what we need. Also, prayer brings us into submission to the will of God. Most Christians will readily admit they are glad God has not answered all their prayers. He knows what we need better than we do.

It's great just to sit down and say to God, "Here's what I'm thinking and feeling, Lord, about the things that I'm dealing with in my life. I know You know everything about me, so I bring all my thoughts and preferences and desires and lay them before You. Help me sort them out and choose wisely. I know You will guide me and not let me make a foolish mistake, because I willingly submit my will to Yours in these matters. Thank You for knowing everything about my life."

GOD'S OMNISCIENCE AND OUR SUFFERING

We long the most for someone to talk to when we are suffering. And yet, sometimes, our pain is so profound that we don't know how to express it even to a person who is close to us and who is willing to listen. The blessing of knowing an all-knowing God is two-fold: He is willing to hear us when we cry; but beyond that, He knows our heart-cry even when we can't find words to express it. God has observed us as we have gone through the experience, so He knows the source of our pain. He can read our heart and mind to know just how we feel in spite of our inability to put it into words.

Psalm 31:7 says, "I will be glad and rejoice in Your mercy, for You have considered my trouble; You have known my soul in adversities." And Psalm 142:3 says, "When my spirit was overwhelmed within me, then You knew my path."

God knows what we experience. He knows every minute of our pain and suffering. He not only knows what we feel, He knows why we feel what we feel. He knows how it happened, and how long it's going to last, and how intense it is. He knows every motion that's associated with it. And when you're going through difficult times, sometimes all you can do is look up and say, "Father, You know."

GOD'S OMNISCIENCE AND OUR FELLOWSHIP WITH HIM

The Bible says God knows those who are His (2 Timothy 2:19) and that He knows the way of the righteous (Psalm 1:6). Those verses suggest the part of God's omniscience I like the best—how it impacts my daily fellowship with Him. God is the best, perfect friend all of us have ever longed for. He never takes things the wrong way or misunderstands what we say or do. There's nothing He can discover about us which would make Him love us any less.

Did you hear about the wealthy grandfather who purchased a new, hi-tech hearing aid? After using it a couple of weeks, he stopped back by the store where he had purchased it and told the manager he could not only hear normal conversations but things being said in the next room as well. "Your family and relatives must be delighted at how well you can hear now," the proprietor said. "Oh, I haven't told them yet," the grandfather said. "I've just been sitting around listening. And I've changed my will four times this week already!"

God is not like that, waiting to catch us saying something wrong, nor do we have to speak loudly and clearly lest He not hear us. God never changes His "will" based on our behavior. He already knows us and loves us perfectly in spite of what He knows. No bad report from the tale-bearer or news of our failures or indiscretions will take God by surprise. He already knows it all.

We spend so much time longing for transparency and intimacy... longing for someone with whom we can share our thoughts and dreams... someone who will understand us even when we are confused about what we say or feel. We want someone who will accept our good thoughts and our bad, someone in whose presence we would have no fear at all. We say, "I would spend every moment I could with such a person if I could only find him. I would live in the safety of that person's understanding and acceptance. I would tell that person everything I'm afraid to tell everyone else." You can see where I am going with this, can't you? We have such a person in God. In fact, He already knows all the things within us that we are aching to talk to someone about—*He already knows them!*

Our challenge is to recognize that God is the partner we've been longing for and begin to dwell in His presence, accepting His acceptance of us.

God knows me and He knows you. He knows everything we've ever done right and everything we've ever done wrong—every righteous thought and every unrighteous thought. And here's what else He knows: He knows that I am "accepted in the Beloved" (Ephesians 1:6), that I have been declared righteous through the blood of Jesus Christ. He knows that I stand holy in the presence of God through His Son, Jesus Christ. And though He sees all of my error and failure and sin, He sees it through the lens of His grace that declares me positionally and eternally holy in His sight. I have been chosen in Christ before the foundation of the world was laid, and I stand holy before God. And if you know Jesus Christ, you stand holy before God.

God is the only person who can see us as we are in the flesh and as we are in Christ at the same time, and the only person who will choose to walk with us unconditionally day after day.

GOD'S OMNISCIENCE AND OUR SIN

It would be nice to stop our lesson on God's omniscience at the end of that last point; but to be faithful to the Word of God, we have to talk about omniscience and sin. Sin—we hardly ever hear that three-letter word mentioned these days. It seems we're more comfortable calling it "moral failure" or "conditioned response to our environment" or "predisposed behavior."

Because God is omniscient, He knows our sins. There is nothing hidden from Him in all of creation, and it is to Him that all men will give an accounting (Psalm 44:21; 69:5; 90:8; Hebrews 4:13). There are no secret thoughts or secret plans or secret longings or secret fears. There are no secrets from God, period. Every thought that flashes through our mind is visible to the eye of God. If we have committed secret sins or secret crimes, God knows every detail of them. None of our excuses will hold water before Him because He knows the pure facts about every situation. God is the judge and jury in both time and eternity. We have not gotten away with anything that we think we have.

How would you feel if, some Sunday morning, every thought that crossed your mind for the last seven days were revealed in foot-high letters on a large screen in the front of your church? If you're like me, you shudder at the very thought of such a thing! I wouldn't want my thoughts for the last day, much less seven, revealed to anyone. And yet they are revealed to God.

Maybe it's just me, but it seems from my observations as I travel about the country that children are getting less and less fearful of disobeying their parents in public—right in front of anyone who might happen to be watching. Someone has written that "it is a hardened child who flaunts his rebellious way in front of his parents." It seems children used to make every effort to commit their acts of disobedience behind their parents' backs, but that has changed. We cringe in shame and sorrow for both parent and child when we see brazen acts of disobedience take place. And yet, do we not act just as brazenly when we sin in plain view of our Heavenly Father?

One day, every Christian will stand before Jesus Christ to acknowledge that which God has known all of our lives. Our character will be revealed (not our reputation), and our rewards in Christ will be determined by what God sees. If you are in Christ, you will be saved, though perhaps with a measure of shame. Except for the blood of Jesus Christ that cleanses us from our sin, we could not be saved at all.

May God's omniscience be a comfort in our hour of need and a motivator in our hour of temptation. May we love all the more the One who loves us in spite of all He knows.

PERSONAL QUESTIONS

1. Read Matthew 6:32.

   a. Since God knows our every need, why do we still need to pray?

   b. Are you grateful God hasn't given you everything you've asked of Him? Why do you think He hasn't?

   c. What do you usually bring before God through prayer? Do you listen to what He has to tell you?

2. Have you ever been in a time of pain that was so hurtful you couldn't express it to the one you knew best? If so, what made it difficult to share that pain with someone?

   a. Have you ever wished that someone knew how you were feeling without having to explain it?

   b. In Psalm 142:3, what did the psalmist experience when his spirit was overwhelmed?

   c. What can you do to stay focused on God when you're going through difficult times?

3. Read 2 Timothy 2:19.

   a. Is it comforting to be known as one of God's own?

   b. Because He is in fellowship with us, do you think God ever takes things the wrong way or misunderstands us?

   c. Have you ever tried to explain yourself to God, thinking maybe He doesn't have the right idea about your intentions?

1. God is all-knowing. What are the different ways these writers express God's omniscience? Discuss together as a group.

   a. Job 37:16

   b. Psalm 147:4

   c. Matthew 10:29-30

2. Psalm 139:16 says God knows all the days of our life—"the days fashioned for [us]."

   a. Considering this truth, is God ever surprised by what occurs to us?

   b. Does understanding that God is all-knowing make you feel safe or scared?

3. God is always aware of our needs (Matthew 6:32), so why must we pray to Him? Share your thoughts with the group.

4. Read Psalm 44:21 and 69:5 together.

   a. Are there any secrets or sins that God does not know about?

   b. Are there things you had hoped to keep secret from God?

c. What is your initial reaction to being exposed to the Creator of the universe?

d. How does knowing that God is omniscient make you want to live your life? Share your answers with the group.

5. Read Hebrews 4:13 as a group.

a. Knowing that nothing is hidden from God, what does your frame of mind have to be in order to continue sinning in front of Him?

b. What must Christians do one day before the Lord?

DID YOU KNOW?

The "omni-" words in a Christian theology—*omnipresent* (everywhere present), *omniscient* (all-knowing), *omnipotent* (all-powerful)—are used legitimately only with reference to God, not Satan. Many mistakenly believe that Satan, as the enemy of God and a powerful spiritual being, has many of the same attributes of God. Satan is not all-knowing, nor is he all-powerful, nor can he be present everywhere at once. Satan is an angel, a created being, with all the limitations of angelic beings created by God for service in heaven and on earth. Granted, he was, at one time, a highly ranked angel, and by virtue of his original anointing has great strength and cunning. But he in no way has the same eternal and infinite characteristics related to space and time, knowledge, and power that God has. It is because of Satan's limitations and his subjection to God's unlimited authority that Christians can resist him and see him flee (James 4:7).

KNOWING A SOVEREIGN GOD

Daniel 4:35

In this lesson we learn the proper response to the sovereign God of the universe.

If you were to walk into a public high school today and see armed policemen patrolling the halls, you would ask, "What happened to the school authorities?" One place you won't find armed guards is in the halls of the universe. God has been, and remains, firmly in control of our world.

I. **Because God Is Sovereign, I Will Reverence Him**

II. **Because God Is Sovereign, I Will Respond to Him in Obedience**

III. **Because God Is Sovereign, I Will Worship Him**

I remember when the California legislature passed the "three strikes" law for repeat offenders (three strikes and you're off to jail). The same week that "get tough on crime" legislation passed, the California legal system released a convicted child molester who had scores of convictions back on the streets. I remember thinking to myself, "Who's in control here?"

That question is going to become more and more important in the days ahead for people who live in our world. Increasingly, people who have trusted in man's structures to bring order and civility to life are losing hope. Man's ability to provide a stable environment seems to be eluding his grasp. Christians are not surprised at that fact since we know that man, in and of himself, is out of control. For us, the question of "Who's in control?" has a very simple answer: God is!

The theological term we use when we talk about God being in control is *sovereignty*. That term means that God is subject to no one, influenced by no one, and absolutely independent and free in His own being. He does as He pleases—only, always, wherever, and forever as He pleases. No one can hinder Him or compel Him to stop. God is sovereign and in control of the universe He created.

God's sovereignty means He is the highest authority in the universe. He does what He wills in heaven and on earth. No one can question Him and say, "Why are You doing what You are doing?" God is the Governor over all the nations, King over all kings, and true Lord over all would-be-lords. That is how the Bible presents God as the sovereign of the universe.

I have found more than forty passages of Scripture that declare the truth of God's sovereignty. While I cannot discuss them all in this lesson, I do want to highlight a few.

- Psalm 22:28: "For the kingdom is the Lord's, and He rules over the nations."
- Psalm 33:11: "The counsel of the Lord stands forever, the plans of His heart to all generations."
- Psalm 50:11-12: "I know all the birds of the mountains, and the wild beasts of the field are Mine.... and all its fullness."
- Psalm 99:1: "The Lord reigns; let the peoples tremble!"
- Psalm 103:19: "The Lord has established His throne in heaven, and His kingdom rules over all."
- Psalm 115:3: "But our God is in heaven; He does whatever He pleases."

- Psalm 135:6: "Whatever the Lord pleases He does, in heaven and in earth, in the seas and in all deep places."

Other passages which teach the sovereignty of God are Deuteronomy 10:17; Proverbs 19:21; 21:30; Isaiah 14:27; 45:9; 46:10; Jeremiah 27:5; Daniel 4:17, 35; Acts 17:24-26.

Along with the doctrine of sin, we hear little preaching about the sovereignty of God (I wonder if there is a connection?). In prior generations it was a familiar topic for preachers. I looked up "sovereignty" in the index to the collected works of the great nineteenth-century London preacher Charles Haddon Spurgeon. Judging from the copious references, one would think he preached on God's sovereignty every other week! Spurgeon, along with many preachers of his era, was captivated by the truth of the sovereignty of God. He must have seen it as a central truth to be expounded when preaching the Gospel: God is in charge of this world and it is to Him that all men must one day give an account.

Here's a statement Spurgeon made in one of his sermons concerning God's sovereignty.

There is no doctrine more hated by the worldlings, no truth of which they have made such a foot-ball, as the great, stupendous, yet most certain doctrine of the Sovereignty of the infinite Jehovah. Men will allow God to be everywhere except on his throne. They will allow him to be in his workshop to fashion the worlds and make the stars. . . . They will allow him to sustain heaven and earth and bear up the pillars thereof, or light the lamps of heaven, or rule the waves of the ever-moving ocean; but when God ascends to his throne, his creatures then gnash their teeth; and when we proclaim an enthroned God, and his right to do as he wills with his own, to dispose of his creatures as he thinks well, without consulting them in the matter, then it is that we are hissed and execrated, and then it is that men turn a deaf ear to us, for God on his throne is not the God they love.

Preach on the love, grace, and mercy of God, and men will applaud. But preach on His sovereignty, and they will recoil. Man does not like to hear that he is not in charge. Today, more than at any time in recorded history, is the day of "almighty man." It is the age of secular humanism. Man, through science and technology, is trying to take destiny into his own hands. At a time when man has set himself up as a little god, he is not likely to be eager to hear the message of the sovereignty of the true God.

Attempts to abolish capital punishment are an example of the little gods trying to usurp authority from the true God. The murder of unborn children is another example; the abolition of marriage and family, yet another. Removing references to God from public classrooms is a fourth example, and the normalization of sodomy and sexual perversion, a fifth. God's law says one thing; man's law says another. God says, "This is how it must be," and man says, "Sorry, we prefer a different way. We don't want God to rule over us."

The world ought to step back and ask itself the question, "How are we doing solving the world's problems our own way? What success have we had in disavowing God's sovereign right to rule over us?" The conclusion would have to be, "Man has not been very successful." We've polluted our world so that even our water and food supplies are tainted with poisons and carcinogens. Our world is shaken by wars and terrorist attacks on a daily basis. Our economy is a source of insecurity. Doomsday weapons exist in the hands of unstable governments. You would think that reasonable people might begin to wonder whether there is not a better way, whether rejecting God is such a good idea after all. The world is living like a man who, having lost his road map, increases his speed. He only arrives at the wrong place faster.

Granted, Bible readers have an advantage. We can look back in the Scriptures and see the many times man rejected God and ended up in trouble. Skipping over the obvious example of Adam and Eve, we can point out Nimrod who gathered the people together to build a great tower as a manifestation of human sovereignty (Genesis 11). Later in Genesis, there's the story of Jacob's sons who got rid of their brother Joseph because they didn't like the idea of him one day ruling over them. Then, years later, it is that very brother who, as the prime minister of Egypt, saved their lives during a famine. Joseph told them about their evil act: "You meant evil against me; but God meant it for good" (Genesis 50:20). During the captivity of the Jews in Persia, an evil man named Haman plotted to destroy the Jews and any record of their God. He built a gallows to hang one of the Jewish leaders, Mordecai, but ended up being hanged on it himself—and the Jews were exalted by the king.

In Egypt, Pharaoh commanded that all the newborn Hebrew boys be thrown into the Nile River. And God used that very Nile River to hide the Hebrew child, Moses, who grew up to lead the Hebrew slaves to freedom. Pharaoh shook his hand in God's face and refused to let the slaves go, finally agreeing after his country had been decimated by ten plagues. But as soon as the Hebrews had left Egypt, Pharaoh came after them with a vengeance and trapped them on the shore of the Red Sea. The Red Sea, which had been a barrier to their escape, parted for the Israelites and then closed over the pursuing Egyptian soldiers. The great body of water that Pharaoh thought would be a trap for the Israelites became a trap for his own army.

Throughout history, whenever man has tried to assert his influence and control, he has been confounded by the sovereign plan of God.

Thinking of it this way helps me: When several thousand people go aboard one of the giant cruise ships for a vacation, or an ocean crossing, they each enter the boat with their own "sovereign" agendas. Each has a story to tell and a mission to fulfill. But guess how much control they actually have over the destination of that giant ship? None. The captain is in charge. Oh, they may act like they're in control in their own little cabin, but their cabin goes where the captain says it should go. Wherever he points the ship, all the hundreds of cabins, and the thousands of people in them, go. So who's really in charge?

I've identified three responses that I believe every Christian should have to the doctrine of the sovereignty of God.

BECAUSE GOD IS SOVEREIGN, I WILL REVERENCE HIM

What would happen in your church on a given Sunday morning if a note were delivered to the pastor at the beginning of the service saying the President of the United States had just arrived and would like to worship with your church? Regardless of your views on any particular president's policies, I would hope your church would rise to its feet as the President entered and make him welcome with all due respect. He is, after all, the highest authority in our land (Romans 13:1).

If we accord to the President of the United States, a frail and sinful human being, respect and honor, how much more should we give respect and reverence to the sovereign ruler of the universe, Jesus Christ—the Lord of lords and King of kings? With the doctrine of the sovereignty of God should come a new sense of fear, honor, and reverence for the one who is sovereign over all earthly and spiritual rulers.

We don't hear the phrase "God-fearing man or woman" much anymore, do we? In generations past, there was a much healthier sense of the necessity for "the fear of God" than there is today. After all, Proverbs says the fear of the Lord is the beginning of knowledge (1:7) and wisdom (9:10). There is, no doubt, a direct correlation between our waywardness as a culture and our having forgotten the necessity for fearing (respecting, honoring, standing in awe of) the Lord. Anyone who is a Christian ought to be characterized by the fear of the Lord. It is the only appropriate response to the One who is *the* sovereign ruler of the universe.

Because God Is Sovereign, I Will Respond to Him in Obedience

Had we been in Pharaoh's court the day Moses and Aaron first walked in and demanded the release of the Hebrew slaves, we might have chuckled to ourselves. Who was this dusty shepherd from Midian to tell Pharaoh what to do with the slaves that were his "property"? Here is how Pharaoh responded: "Who is the Lord, that I should obey His voice to let Israel go? I do not know the Lord, nor will I let Israel go" (Exodus 5:2).

To be fair, it's not hard to understand why Pharaoh answered disobediently. He didn't know who *Yahweh*, the Lord God of Israel, was. How would you act if someone came to your door and said, "In the name of the god Marduk, I order you to turn over your property to me"? You probably would dial 911 after closing and locking your door! If someone doesn't know the legitimacy of a god or ruler, we wouldn't expect him to obey.

Conversely, if one does know the legitimacy of a god or ruler, wouldn't we expect that person to obey instantly—or at least in a fashion commensurate with the god's or ruler's authority? Absolutely. Therefore, given the fact that Christians confess to know the one true God and acknowledge His sovereignty over all, wouldn't we expect Christians to respond instantly and obediently to everything God says? You would think so, but such is not always the case.

Any Christian who believes that the God of the Bible, the God of Abraham, Isaac, and Jacob, the God and Father of our Lord Jesus Christ is the true sovereign God of the universe… that Christian has to read the Bible and engage in prayer not just as spiritual exercises but as a means of finding out what the sovereign God would have him to do. A good example of submission to the will of God is the priest Eli in the Old Testament. When Eli heard from Samuel that God was going to kill his two rebellious sons, Eli said, "It is the Lord. Let Him do what seems good to Him." Wow! That's submission to a difficult word, isn't it? That ought to be the response of every believer to the Lord's directives for his life.

Because God Is Sovereign, I Will Worship Him

The last dream King David had for Israel was that he be allowed to build a temple for God in Jerusalem. But God came to David near the end of his life and told him that because he had been a man of war and bloodshed in his life, he would not be allowed to build God's house, a house of peace (1 Chronicles 28:3). While brokenhearted, David received that word from God submissively; he prepared his son, Solomon, to build the temple instead.

So, instead of building the temple, David took on the task of chief fundraiser. He not only gave generously from his own resources, he led the campaign by which all Israel contributed vast amounts of money for the temple project (1 Chronicles 29:1-9). David prayed a powerful prayer (29:10-19) in which he worshiped the Lord for providing the funds to build the temple. He recognized that everything given by every person came first from the hand of a sovereign God to whom all things ultimately belong.

David's understanding of the sovereignty of God led him to worship the sovereign God. If he couldn't worship Him by building Him a temple, he would worship Him by providing the resources—and then praising Him for making the resources possible.

Reverence, obedience, and worship are three characteristics of the believer who responds to God as the sovereign He is.

1. What does the term *sovereignty* mean?

    a. What does it mean in relation to God?

    b. Read Psalm 22:28 and 33:11. Do these verses give you a clearer picture of God's sovereignty? Why or why not?

2. Why do you think mankind is so intent on doing things their own way?

    a. What do people often do to show their independence from God? Are they successful?

    b. How do you rate in this area? Is it easy, difficult, or seemingly impossible for you to submit to God?

3. Turn to the section titled, "Because God Is Sovereign, I Will Reverence Him."

    a. Read Proverbs 9:10. What marks the beginning of wisdom?

b. There is a correlation between our _____ and our having forgotten _____.

c. In what ways can we show reverence to God?

4. Read 1 Chronicles 28:2-6.

   a. Why did God not allow David to build the temple?

   b. What did David do instead?

   c. Do you ever feel inspired to worship as David did, thinking of the sovereignty of God?

5. Is God in charge of you? Do you acknowledge His right to rule and reign in your life? Are there any issues you are struggling with right now concerning God's way versus your way? If so, what are they?

1. As a group discuss the definition of the term *sovereignty* as defined in this lesson.

2. Read the following verses together and discuss the ways in which God's sovereignty is described.

    a. Psalm 33:11

    b. Psalm 99:1

    c. Psalm 135:6

3. Who is the most powerful person you know? What do you think your response would be if that person asked you to do something?

    a. What was Pharaoh's response when Moses and Aaron demanded the release of the Hebrew slaves? (Exodus 5:2)

b. What is your usual reaction to authority? Do you respond the same way to earthly authority as you do to heavenly authority?

c. How do you think you can learn to resign yourself to God's will?

d. Do you believe rejoicing is an end result of knowing that God's will is done, that God is in charge? Why or why not?

4. Discuss the three characteristics of the believer who responds to God as the sovereign He is.

5. What is your biggest takeaway from this lesson? What did you learn about the sovereignty of God that you previously did not know? Share your answers with the group.

The word *sovereign* derives from a root which means "about others." Our English word comes from the Old French *souverein*, "ruler," which hearkens back to the Latin *super*, "above." In 1498, King Henry VII of England introduced the sovereign, a magnificent gold coin, into the monetary system of England. On the front of the coin was the image of Henry VII seated on an elaborate throne, suitable for a "sovereign" ruler of the land, the ruler above all others. Though the sovereign is no longer a British coin, the worth of the coin in terms of gold was applied in 1817 to a gold coin worth one pound—still the denomination in England "above" all other coins.

KNOWING AN EVER-PRESENT GOD

Psalm 139:7-8

In this lesson we discover the benefits of God always being with us.

OUTLINE

The age we live in has made it possible for us to extend our influence around the world: phone calls, email, video conferencing, and, one day, holograms. But that's not the same as God's omnipresence. Only He can give all of Himself to an infinite number of situations simultaneously.

I. **Meditate on This Truth When You Need Conviction to Face Temptation**

II. **Meditate on This Truth When You Need Courage to Face Difficulty**

III. **Meditate on This Truth When You Need Confidence to Face Hard Assignments**

The late, great theologian Francis Schaeffer wrote a book that has become a classic in Christian theology titled *The God Who Is There*. It was a powerful defense of the existence of God and the implication for those who say they believe in Him. We could easily rephrase the title of Schaeffer's book for this lesson and call it, "The God Who Is Here, There, and Everywhere." That truly describes the God of Scripture, the omnipresent God—the God who is everywhere at once.

God is, at the same time, present with His whole being in every part of the universe yet present in different ways in different places. We struggle with that concept because we are spatial creatures, fixed to a particular place in space and time. While we may think we are in two places at once via such devices as video conferencing, "we" are not really there. An image of us is not the same thing as us being there.

Dietrich Ritchel wrote of an experience he had in World War II in Germany. His city was destroyed by Allied bombs. After one particular bombing wave was over, he looked up at the roof of the partially destroyed railroad station and caught a glimpse of an inscription: "Beyond the stars there must live a gracious Father" written in German. He said out loud to himself, "I do not want such a God. I do not want a God who is beyond the stars. I want a God who is here, a God who is present, a God who is available, a God who knows and understands my situation."

Certainly that is what everyone wants—a God who dwells with us and understands what we are going through. And that is certainly what we have in Jesus Christ, the God of the universe who came to dwell among us (John 1:14).

The Scriptures give ample testimony to the omnipresence of God and how He fills the universe with His presence. A key text about God's omnipresence is 1 Kings 8:27: "But will God indeed dwell on the earth? Behold, heaven and the heaven of heavens cannot contain You. How much less this temple which I have built!" The setting was the completion of the grand temple that Solomon built for God in Jerusalem. It was huge —and magnificent! And yet Solomon understood that, as great as the temple was, it could not contain God. Indeed, the "heaven of heavens," the highest heavens, are not sufficient to contain God. We wonder how that is possible until we remember that God created the universe— that is, He is outside the universe in terms of His "size," immensity, and presence. He fills the universe and beyond.

Psalm 139:7-10 may be the most well-known text on God's omnipresence. The version of this text in the New Living Translation puts it wonderfully:

I can never escape from your Spirit!
I can never get away from your presence!
If I go up to heaven, you are there;
if I go down to the grave, you are there.
If I ride the wings of the morning,
if I dwell by the farthest oceans,
even there your hand will guide me,
and your strength will support me.

And Jeremiah 23:23-24 records God asking questions about His own presence, this from the New International Version:

"Am I only a God nearby,"
declares the Lord,
"and not a God far away?
Who can hide in secret places
so that I cannot see them?"
declares the Lord.
"Do not I fill heaven and earth?"
declares the Lord.

In this day of New Age heresy, it is important to note a distinction between omnipresence and pantheism—an Eastern religious philosophy that sounds biblical, but is not. Pantheism says their god is everywhere because their god is everything. Wherever space, time, and matter exist in the universe, God is there because all matter is God. That certainly is not what the Bible teaches. God is a person, not a rock or a chair or a tree. God is everywhere in creation, but He is not the creation. He is separate and distinct from that which He has created.

God is everywhere all the time, but His presence is manifested in different ways in different places and times. That's why you can come away from church or a concert or conference and say, "I really sensed the presence of the Lord in that place." Or we may sense the closeness of the Lord with us when we go through difficulties and suffering.

Psalm 139:8 says, "If I make my bed in hell, behold, You are there." And Psalm 22:3 says God is "enthroned in the praises of Israel." Are we to believe that God's presence is the same in hell as amidst the praises of Israel, His people? No, but the Bible says He is present in both, just in different ways.

I have found in my own spiritual life that meditating upon different aspects of God's eternal character provides significant comfort and help in different times of my life. During times of change and upheaval, I can meditate on the immutability of God—the fact that He never changes. If I fail or struggle with sin, I can meditate on the mercy of God. And there is a time when the omnipresence of God provides strength: when I am facing temptation.

MEDITATE ON THIS TRUTH WHEN YOU NEED CONVICTION TO FACE TEMPTATION

Think about this: You have a friend who, in a moment of weakness, is being sorely tempted to do something he knows is wrong. Not maybe wrong, but definitely, big-time wrong. Imagine saying to that person, "You can go ahead and do this thing, but I just want you to know that God is supposed to be arriving here on the scene in a matter of moments." What do you think your friend would do? Would he forge ahead and commit the sin, or would he take a rain check: "Well, if God is going to be here, I guess I could always put this off until tomorrow or the next day."

Even a person who doesn't have a high view of God would have a hard time committing an obvious sin in the immediate presence of God. And yet people do it every day, even people who have a high view of God like you and me!

Meditating on the truth of God's omnipresence is a great antidote to the temptation to sin. Why? Because it reminds us that God is always present—just as much as if He were standing next to us as a physical person. Most people would hesitate to sin in the immediate presence of a friend or family member, yet we are willing to do so in the presence of God. We can't have God for comfort and then deny His ministry of conviction. If you want Him to be with you for one, you'll have to accept His presence for the other.

It's interesting, if not amusing, to see Adam and Eve hiding from God in the Garden of Eden after they sinned (Genesis 3:8). Hiding from God in His own garden! Did they think God did not know where they were, or was not aware they had sinned? Perhaps they didn't know Him very well at that point, but there is no hiding from God.

And think about Jonah, whom God commissioned to go and preach repentance to the Ninevites. He went down to the coastline in Israel and hopped on a sailing ship heading west toward Tarshish (Spain). Bad move. Did Jonah think God wasn't able to follow him across the ocean? That God wouldn't find him in Tarshish? It says in Jonah 1:10 that Jonah told the sailors on the ship that he was fleeing from the presence of the Lord. It's obvious that Jonah thought he could run fast and far enough to get outside the boundaries of God's presence. The sailors apparently had more wisdom than Jonah did, blaming him for the storm that came up—so they threw him overboard, hoping the God he was running from would still the stormy sea. God found Jonah in the ocean and sequestered him for three days in the belly of a giant fish where Jonah discovered it was impossible to flee from the presence of God.

Dutch theologian Hermann Bobbink has pictured beautifully what happens when we try to get alone to sin:

> When you wish to do something evil, you retire from public into your house, alone, where no enemy can see. And from these places in your house which are open and visible to the eyes of men, you retire yourself to your room. And even in your room, you fear some witness from another quarter, so you retire yourself into your heart. And when you get into your heart, there He is already.

If I will remember that God is wherever I am, I will have the conviction I need to face and flee from temptation.

MEDITATE ON THIS TRUTH WHEN YOU NEED COURAGE TO FACE DIFFICULTY

One of the most powerful passages in the Bible on God's presence in times of difficulty is worth our attention (Isaiah 43:1-3, 5).

> But now, thus says the Lord, who created you, O Jacob,
> And He who formed you, O Israel:
> "Fear not, for I have redeemed you;
> I have called you by your name;
> You are Mine.
> When you pass through the waters, I will be with you;
> And through the rivers, they shall not overflow you.
> When you walk through the fire, you shall not be burned,
> Nor shall the flame scorch you.
> For I am the Lord your God,
> The Holy One of Israel, your Savior;
> I gave Egypt for your ransom,
> Ethiopia and Seba in your place....
>
> Fear not, for I am with you."

God's presence is always with us, but He manifests Himself at different times—especially when we are going through the deep waters of life. I have said, and have heard others say, "That was one of the most difficult experiences I've ever been through, but God was more real to me during that time than I've ever known Him to be before." God is not more present with us during times of trouble, but the manifestation (the manifest presence) of God is often more real.

If troubles in life are difficult, they can't compare to the end of life —walking through the valley of the shadow of death. And yet the psalmist David said he would "fear no evil; for You are with me" when death looms large.

MEDITATE ON THIS TRUTH WHEN YOU NEED CONFIDENCE TO FACE HARD ASSIGNMENTS

You and I both fall into the category of people who have faced challenging assignments from God that we felt completely unqualified to handle. Sometimes God's leading is unmistakable, but our natural reaction is sheer terror—"Lord, choose someone else!"

That was how Moses felt when God called him to be the deliverer of the Hebrew slaves from Egypt. Moses, an eighty-year-old shepherd in Midian, is told by God that he is going to confront the most powerful ruler in the world and demand that he let God's people go. How would you have felt? Probably exactly like Moses felt—not excited at all about the prospects of surviving.

But in Exodus 3:12, we find that God answers all of Moses' objections with a simple statement: "I will certainly be with you." Would that have been enough assurance for you or for me? It should be. If God promises to be with us, that's all we need to know. Without that assurance, we could not fault Moses if he had turned down the assignment. There have been plenty of things I have been faced with tackling which, had I not known God was going to be with me, I would have declined to undertake. There's a huge difference between tackling something impossible alone and tackling something impossible with God by your side.

Moses was successful, as we know; and near the end of his life, when it was time to turn over his leadership responsibilities to Joshua, Moses gave his protégé this word of encouragement: "And the Lord, He is the One who goes before you. He will be with you, He will not leave you nor forsake you; do not fear nor be dismayed" (Deuteronomy 31:8). Moses had learned a life-changing leadership lesson as the rescuer of Israel from Egypt: If God is with you, you can do anything He asks of you.

Then there was Gideon, called by God to deliver the Israelites from the Midianites. God finds Gideon hiding from the enemy—not exactly the profile of a great military deliverer. But God spoke to Gideon from His perspective—the person we know Gideon could become: "The Lord is with you, you mighty man of valor!" (Judges 6:12) I can see Gideon looking around and saying, "Who, me?" And Gideon did deliver Israel from the Midianites because God was with him.

And don't forget about Jeremiah, the prophet to Judah and Jerusalem. God told him that he would be sent to the nations to speak

God's Word. When Jeremiah objected that he was only a youth, God said, "Do not be afraid of their faces, for I am with you to deliver you" (Jeremiah 1:8).

All through Scripture, the primary supporting element for those called to do difficult things for God was God's presence with them. Maybe we ought to make that our primary resource when we ask people to undertake difficult tasks: "I know this is a tough assignment, and I can only promise you this: God will be with you." I remember how scared I was when God called me to be the pastor where I currently serve. For weeks, I was petrified, even though I didn't say so. The only reason I survived then and have survived until now is that I could hear God telling me, "I didn't call you to do this by yourself. I'm going to be with you." And He was—and is.

You may be wrestling right now with an assignment God has set before you. But let me tell you this: Your feelings of insecurity and incapability are probably a good indication that you should do it. I have found that God normally calls us to things that are beyond our ability in order that we will turn to Him and trust Him. Why would we need Him if it was something we could do ourselves? What growth would there be in doing something we're entirely capable of doing?

Take to heart this often-repeated quote: "Attempt something so great for God that it is doomed to fail unless God is in it." If God has called you to it, I promise He will be with you. And God does not fail in what He purposes to accomplish.

Remember one of the last things Jesus told His disciples: "Lo, I am with you always, even to the end of the age" (Matthew 28:20).

PERSONAL QUESTIONS

1. God's Word tells us there is no place we can go where God is not present. Read the following verses and list the different ways God's omnipresence is expressed.

   a. Psalm 139:7-10

   b. Jeremiah 23:23-24

2. Read Genesis 3:4-8.

   a. Have you ever tried to hide from God like Adam and Eve did?

   b. If so, in what way?

3. In Jonah 1:10, how did Jonah flee from the presence of the Lord?

   a. Do you know anyone who is running away from God?

   b. What happens in those cases?

4. Read Isaiah 43:1-5.

   a. Are you going through any difficulties in your life right now?

   b. What does the Lord say He will do when you face difficulties? (verse 2)

   c. What does He say in verse 5?

   d. Has there been a difficult time when you felt God's presence? If so, how was it manifested?

5. Turn to the section titled, "Meditate on This Truth When You Need Confidence to Face Hard Assignments."

   a. What is the primary supporting element for those who are called to do difficult things for the Lord?

   b. Does God ever fail to accomplish His purposes?

   c. What will the Lord do, even until the end of time? (Matthew 28:20)

GROUP QUESTIONS

1. How does it make you feel to know we have an ever-present God? Discuss.

   a. Does God's omnipresence ever confuse you? Why or why not?

   b. How does John 1:14 help us to understand His omnipresence?

   c. What can we learn from Psalm 139:7-10 and Jeremiah 23:23-24? Is there anywhere we can go where God is not present?

2. Even though we have a high view of God, we can be tempted to sin. Why do you think this is?

   a. How is meditating on God's truth a great antidote to the temptation to sin?

   b. Have you ever tried to hide your sin from God? What happened?

3. One of the consistent patterns in the Bible concerning God's omniscience occurs when God gives assignments to people. Read the following verses and describe how God reiterates this.

   a. Exodus 3:11-12

   b. Deuteronomy 31:7-8

4. Is there an assignment that you feel God wants you to undertake? How does knowing God is with you change your outlook at times like these?

5. Discuss as a group the ways meditating on God's truth can enhance your spiritual life.

DID YOU KNOW?

When the Russian cosmonaut Yuri Gagarin became the first person to travel in space in 1961, he returned to earth and declared that God must not exist because he didn't see Him anywhere in space. When Frank Borman commanded the first American astronaut crew to travel beyond earth's orbit, he read from Genesis 1, from 250,000 miles in space, "In the beginning, God created the heavens and the earth." Later he said, "I had an enormous feeling … that there was a God, that there was indeed a beginning." When Eugene "Buzz" Aldrin became the second person ever to walk on the moon, before leaving his module for the historic moon walk, he took out some items he had smuggled on board: a Bible, silver chalice, and sacramental bread and wine. James Irwin walked on the moon in 1971 and said, "I felt the power of God as I'd never felt it before." Charles Duke followed Irwin to the moon and said when he returned, "I make speeches about walking *on* the moon and walking *with* the Son." Given the number of astronauts who have encountered God in outer space, the original Russian cosmonaut should have looked more closely. God really is everywhere.

KNOWING A LOVING GOD

John 3:16

*In this lesson we learn how God has revealed
His love to man.*

OUTLINE

No word in our "feel good" culture is bandied about with as little precision as *love*. We love fast cars, night baseball, and apple pie. But we would likely not die for any of them. Yet that is the quality and character of the love of God: a love that is selfless and sacrificial.

   I. **The Surpassing Quality of God's Love**

  II. **The Surprising Object of God's Love**

 III. **The Sacrificial Price of God's Love**

 IV. **The Serious Offer of God's Love**

  V. **The Selective Choice of God's Love**

 VI. **The Special Promise of God's Love**

VII. **The Satisfying Fulfillment of God's Love**

The Bible says that God "is" three things: God is light, God is spirit, and God is love. First John 4:8 doesn't say, "God is loving." It says, "God is love"—and there is a difference. We might say that a person we know is a "loving" person, and we would understand what that means. But God is not "loving"—He is love. That means the very essence of His nature is love; everything He does is a manifestation of love; and He cannot do anything that is not love.

The Bible says plenty about the love of God:

- His love is knowable and believable, able to be experienced (1 John 4:16).
- He loves us in spite of our sins (Romans 5:8).
- He loved us before we were able to love Him in return (1 John 4:19).
- His love is revealed in His mercy (Ephesians 2:4).
- His love is everlasting, never-ending (Jeremiah 31:3).

Everything good the human race knows how to do, it learned from God, and that is especially true of love. God set the example for how to love by loving us "in spite of." The clearest sign of God-like love is when someone loves another in spite of what they have done wrong, which is how God loves us.

Another sign of God-like love is sacrifice—loving at a loss. I read a story once about a little boy whose sister needed a blood transfusion to live. The boy had suffered and recovered from the same disease and built up immunity to it in his blood. Because they shared the same rare blood type, the little boy was the only donor available. He agreed to donate his own blood so his sister could live. As the nurse put the needle into his arm, the boy watched his blood begin to drain out of his body through the plastic tube. He looked up at the doctor and asked seriously, "Doctor, when do I die?"

Neither the doctor nor the family realized that the little boy thought he was giving up his life—his blood—so his sister could live. But that's what he was prepared to do.

It's hard to imagine a child having that kind of sacrificial love, isn't it? That's about as close to the kind of sacrificial love God has for us that I can imagine. First John 3:16 says, "By this we know love, because He laid down His life for us." We are looking at genuine, sacrificial love when we look at someone willing to give up his life for another person.

The God-like love was not a part of the Greek vernacular until the love of God in Christ was revealed to the world. The Greeks had words for love, but they did not refer to selfless, sacrificial love. *Eros* referred to physical passions (compare our word *erotic*). *Stergo*, a Greek word not appearing in the New Testament, was used by Greeks to refer to a familial kind of love. Finally, *phileo* is a brotherly kind of love (compare the name "Philadelphia, City of Brotherly Love," and the word *philanthropy*, the love of humankind, often expressed through charitable gifts).

There was not a word in common use that could serve to describe selfless, sacrificial love. The Greek word *agape* was pressed into service by the New Testament writers to describe God's love, a kind of love that seeks nothing in return, that seeks only the benefit and well-being of the one loved. God reached down from heaven for our benefit and loved us and saved us in spite of the fact that we had nothing to offer Him in return.

To talk about God's love in the New Testament, almost everyone would turn to John 3:16 as the central verse: "For God so loved the world that He gave His only begotten Son, that whoever believes in Him should not perish but have everlasting life." The verb for "love" in this verse is *agapao*, the verb form of *agape*. John 3:16 is used in so many presentations of the Gospel because it so clearly reflects the nature of God's saving love. I'll never forget learning once how the Gospel is pictured in John 3:16: "For **G**od so loved the world that He gave His **O**nly begotten **S**on, that whoever believes in Him should not **P**erish but have **E**verlasting **L**ife." The whole Gospel in one verse!

Following are seven dimensions of God's *agape* love as revealed in John 3:16.

THE SURPASSING QUALITY OF GOD'S LOVE

The quality of God's love is revealed in the little word *so*. We could read the verse this way: "God loved the world so much that He gave." His love was not passionless or emotionless. He loved "so much." The Roman world was unfamiliar with a love that was so deep and sacrificial that an innocent person would step forward and die for the guilty.

THE SURPRISING OBJECT OF GOD'S LOVE

The world was the object of God's love in Christ: "God so loved the world." Only an *agape* kind of love could have allowed a Jewish writer, the apostle John, to write such a thing. The Jews looked down with disdain on "the world" of Gentiles, yet here a Jewish writer records the fact that God loved everyone in the world in addition to the Jews.

As a teenager who was wrestling with the implication of the Gospel message, I recall wondering how it was possible for one person to die for everyone in the world. When I came to grips with the deity of Christ, it began to make more sense to me. But it is still an amazing concept to consider that one Man loved the entire world and died in its place.

Dying for "the world" would be like saying to your church, "I love this church." And yet each of us longs for a personal experience with that love which was directed toward the whole world. And then I began considering the love of Christ for the one thief on the cross next to Him, the one who asked to be remembered by Christ in His Kingdom. Jesus turned and expressed His world-sized love to that individual man and gave him assurance of his salvation. God in Christ loved the whole world but also loves every individual in the world.

As Augustine wrote, "He loves each one of us as if we were the only one to love."

THE SACRIFICIAL PRICE OF GOD'S LOVE

The high price of God's love was "His only begotten Son." If you have a son, stop and consider this: Is there anyone you love so much in this world that you would sacrifice your son for him? Many have lost sons in military conflicts in service to our country, and that is hard enough. But those deaths are not usually voluntary and not brought about by a decision of the parents. It's almost inconceivable for us to consider the idea of giving up our son to save the life of another person. Yet that is what God did. The story of Abraham being willing to sacrifice the life of his son Isaac is such a powerful one because it makes real something that many only think theoretically about (Genesis 22). What did it mean for God the Father to offer up His only Son as a sacrifice? In the story of Abraham, we have a step-by-step account of the depth of one man's love.

First John 4:9-10 says, "In this the love of God was manifested toward us, that God has sent His only begotten Son into the world, that we might live through Him. In this is love, not that we loved God, but that He loved us and sent His Son to be the propitiation for our sins." And Romans 8:32 says, "He who did not spare His own Son, but delivered Him up for us all."

Both these verses are pictured beautifully on a poster I saw in a Christian bookstore. It shows a close-up picture of Christ's arms spread wide as He hung on the cross, and has this question and answer written on it: "I asked Jesus how much He loved me, and He said, 'This much.' And He stretched out His hands and died."

That's God's love—the most costly demonstration of pure, selfless love the world has ever seen.

THE SERIOUS OFFER OF GOD'S LOVE

The offer of God's love was made to "whoever." God did not offer His love just to the Jews or just to the Gentiles, but to "whoever"—to everybody in the world. Innumerable theological discussions have taken place down through history over the question of who is represented by the "whoever." Did Christ die for the sins of every person in the world or just for the sins of those who would believe in Him?

This is one of those debates where there is less light than heat. But I will say this: The Bible says that Christ "is the propitiation for our sins, and not for ours only but also for the whole world" (1 John 2:2). Enough grace and love was poured out at Calvary to cover the needs of every person in the world. It doesn't matter where you are as you read these words—what part of the world you live in—God loves you and Christ died for you on the cross. The words of the Bible don't seem to make much sense taken any other way.

The "whoever" doesn't refer just to geography or ethnicity. It also refers to "whoever you are in terms of the depth of your sin." If you think you have sinned so much that God's love couldn't be available to you, you're wrong! "Whoever" means "whoever"—no conditions or limitations. The famous Puritan writer Richard Baxter wrote, "If God had said there was mercy for Richard Baxter, I am so vile a sinner that I would have thought He meant some other Richard Baxter. When He said 'whosoever,' I know that includes me, the worst of all Richard Baxters there ever was."

THE SELECTIVE CHOICE OF GOD'S LOVE

The words that follow "whoever" don't limit *to* whom the love of God is offered, but they do define *by* whom it is received and enjoyed: the ones who believe in Christ. The grace of God is *sufficient* for all but is *efficient* only for those who believe in Christ. The offer is to everyone who will receive it. It's as if you walk into a crowded room full of people and announce the offer of a free gift for everyone in the room. The only ones who get to enjoy and benefit from the gift are those who step forward and receive it.

So it is with the Gospel. Those who step forward by faith and receive God's gift, Jesus Christ, are the ones who benefit from it. That doesn't mean the offer wasn't valid for the rest, and it doesn't mean the offer is withdrawn. The offer of salvation in Christ goes forth continually in the present tense for "whoever" will reach out his hand and accept it. Those who reject the gift are still loved by God, and still have a chance to receive it. But until they do, God's gift remains in the "sufficient" category, not the "efficient." "Whoever" includes the whole world, but "whoever believes" excludes those who don't believe from the possibility of benefiting from God's gift.

THE SPECIAL PROMISE OF GOD'S LOVE

The promise associated with the receipt of God's gift of Christ is that whoever believes "should not perish." But what does "perish" mean?

What does it mean to the one receiving God's gift that he will not perish? Some of the cults say that when we die, we die like an animal with no thought of the afterlife. When you perish, that's it—nothing beyond the grave.

The best way I know to describe what "perish" means is to divide a piece of paper in half, writing "Everlasting Life" at the top of one half and "Perish" at the top of the other half. There is no middle ground between the two. These two terms are antonyms, or opposites. If you understand the idea of eternal life, then "perish" is the opposite. Failure to receive the love of God by not believing in Jesus is a failure to receive everlasting life. And a failure to receive everlasting life is to perish. So the promise of God to those who believe is a promise that they will not perish but have everlasting life.

THE SATISFYING FULFILLMENT OF GOD'S LOVE

The ultimate expression of the consummation of God's love is wrapped up in the phrase "eternal life." I find that many Christians are confused about exactly what eternal life is. A larger percentage of Christians would write down this answer if asked to define eternal life: what happens to a Christian after he dies.

That is not eternal life! Eternal life is something you inherit and a reality that begins the moment you believe in Jesus Christ. Eternal life has less to do with the duration of time than it does the quality of life you are living. The day I received Jesus Christ into my life by faith, my life shifted to a higher plane and my eternal life began. People used to put on tombstones "Entered into life," followed by the date of their birth, and "Entered into eternal life" and the date of their death. Unless they accepted Christ the day they died, like the thief on the cross, that's a misuse of the term "eternal life."

Jesus said in John 17:3, "And this is eternal life, that they may know You, the only true God, and Jesus Christ whom You have sent." Therefore, eternal life is knowing the true God and His Son, not the life you move into the day you die. Knowing God is a new kind and quality of life.

Are you looking for life on a higher plane? If you are looking anywhere except in the person of Jesus Christ, you are looking in vain and will not find it. I commend to you "the love of God our Savior," Jesus Christ (Titus 3:4).

1. Read the following verses and describe the love of God found in each.

   a. Jeremiah 31:3

   b. Romans 5:8

   c. 1 John 4:16

2. How do we know love according to 1 John 3:16?

   a. In the New Testament, what Greek word is used to describe God's love?

   b. What are some words you can think of to try to describe the surpassing quality of God's love?

3. Have you ever thought God's love does not include certain segments of the population?

a. Augustine wrote that God loves each of us like we are the only one to love. How does it feel to know the God of this whole world loves you so much?

b. How do you experience God's love?

4. Read Romans 8:31-39.

   a. Make a list of the elements involved in God's love for us according to this passage.

   b. Can anything separate us from God's love? (verses 38-39)

5. Why do you think some people don't accept God's gift?

   a. Have you ever had anyone refuse a gift you gave? What were the reasons given for the refusal?

   b. Whom is the gift of salvation for? What happens to those who do not accept God's gift?

GROUP QUESTIONS

1. Read 1 John 4:8 as a group.

   a. What term describes God?

   b. A person who does not know love, doesn't know Whom?

   c. Can we conclude that mankind has learned how to love from God? How so?

2. The Greeks had three main terms for love before the New Testament term *agape* was pressed into service. Write them down, then describe their differences. Discuss how *agape* is different from these three terms.

   •

   •

   •

3. Read John 3:16 together.

   a. Why do you think this is such a central verse regarding God's love?

   b. How did God express His love for us?

   c. How do you experience God's love in your daily life?

   d. How can you share God's love with others?

4. Read John 17:3.

   a. What is eternal life?

   b. Have you entered into eternal life? If so, have you ever thought of it
      from that perspective—that you have already started the eternal-
      life phase?

   c. What insights does this give you about living with the knowledge
      that God loves and blesses you when you accept His love? Does
      this change the meaning of death for you? How so?

   d. Discuss how understanding eternal life makes a difference in how
      you live each day.

DID YOU KNOW?

The view that Christ did not die for the whole world but only for
those who will believe is a theological view known as "limited
atonement." It is the third, and most debated, in a list of five
cardinal positions coming out of the Protestant Reformation, typically
labeled as Calvinism: Total depravity of man, Unconditional election of
believers, Limited atonement provided by Christ's death, Irresistible
grace of the Holy Spirit in conversion, and Perseverance of the saints in
the faith. A large part of the evangelical Christian church holds to four
of these five points, the question of the extent of the atonement being a
sticking point. John Wesley, father of Methodism, said regarding the
definition of "world" in John 3:16, "[It refers to] all men under heaven;
even those that despise his love, and will for that cause finally perish.
Otherwise, not to believe would be no sin to them."

KNOWING GOD BY NAME

Psalm 23

In this lesson we learn how the names of God reveal who He is.

OUTLINE

The naming of babies has become a modern phenomenon with books, websites, and guides devoted to the topic. But parents can only hope their child will live up to its name. Not so with God. Names were ascribed to Him not on the basis of what He might do, but who He was known to be.

    I. **Jehovah-Rohi: The Lord My Shepherd**

    II. **Jehovah-Jireh: The Lord Shall Provide**

    III. **Jehovah-Rapha: The Lord Who Heals**

    IV. **Jehovah-Nissi: The Lord My Banner**

    V. **Jehovah-M'Kaddesh: The Lord Who Sanctifies**

    VI. **Jehovah-Shalom: The Lord Who Is Peace**

    VII. **Jehovah-Tsidkenu: The Lord Who Is Righteous**

    VIII. **Jehovah-Shammah: The Lord Who Is There**

If you're a parent, you can probably remember a time when one of your children said, "I love you," for no apparent reason. Just out of the blue, they spoke those emotional and loving words in a way that completely caught you off guard. Naturally, most of what we hear from our children is their requests for this and that, and no parent is offended by those petitions. But to hear "I love you" from a child or grandchild—an affirmation of love with no ulterior agenda—is the essence of relationship.

Somehow, I think God must feel the same way. Most of our time communicating with God is spent doing what children do: asking their parents for something they need. In fact, He invites us to bring our requests to Him (Philippians 4:6-7).

In this series of studies, we have been talking about knowing the God we worship: knowing God for who He is more than for what He can do for us. The premise in this series is that we don't say "I love you" to God more than we do because we don't know Him as well as we should. I said in the first lesson that we can only worship someone we love, and we can only love someone we truly know. To know God is to love Him, and to love Him is to worship Him.

Consider these words of Ron Allen, a gifted writer and speaker on the subject of worship.

> What, then, is the essence of worship? It is the celebration of God. When we worship God, we celebrate Him. Worship is not the casual chatter that occasionally drowns out the organ prelude. We celebrate God when we allow the prelude to tune our hearts to the glory of God.
>
> We celebrate God when we join together earnestly in prayer and earnestly in song.
>
> We celebrate God when all of the parts of the service fit together and work to the common end.
>
> We celebrate God when we give to Him hilariously and serve Him with integrity.
>
> We celebrate God when we enjoy and participate in music to His glory.
>
> We celebrate God as we hear His Word gladly and seek to be conformed by it more and more to the image of the Savior.
>
> We celebrate God when we honor His Word with our words.
>
> As a thoughtful gift is a celebration of a birthday... so worship, done rightly, is a celebration of God.

When the Church of Jesus Christ gathers corporately on the Lord's Day, it should be a celebration of our God. Some people don't like to use the word *celebration*, thinking it sounds too boisterous or secular. In truth, it is the perfect word, a word that suggests we get together to "cheer" for our God—for who He is and what He has done. Think of all the things we celebrate in life without a second thought. Why should we not celebrate the existence and presence of our God?

One thing that is obvious from the Old Testament Scriptures is that worshipers knew how to celebrate. There always seemed to be two aspects to their worship. First, they would build an altar—a place to worship and offer sacrifices to God. And second, they would often remember what God had done by giving Him a new name. They didn't change His name. But they did add a special name to help them remember what He had done. And sometimes, God even gave the name Himself.

The special names given to God in the Old Testament always began with Jehovah, the English form of *Yahweh*, the name by which He revealed Himself to Moses (Exodus 3:14). Following Jehovah was a second name, the combination of the two becoming a new name by which they celebrated God. In this lesson we will look at eight of these names, each of which reveals a unique aspect of the character of our God.

JEHOVAH-ROHI: THE LORD MY SHEPHERD

The first name comes from Psalm 23, from one of the most commonly known phrases in the Bible: "The Lord is my shepherd" (verse 1). In the Hebrew text, the name for God in this verse is *Jehovah-Rohi*—or Jehovah My Shepherd.

When we first meet David in the Old Testament, this youngest son of Jesse is in the fields tending the sheep. The prophet Samuel comes to Jesse's house looking for the next king of Israel; and after meeting all of Jesse's sons, knows he hasn't met the future king. Upon inquiry, Jesse remembers there is one more, David, in the fields with the sheep. Samuel says to send for him, and the shepherd boy is anointed as the next king of Israel.

David knew exactly what it meant to be a shepherd. In fact, even after being anointed by Samuel, he returned to being a shepherd until it was God's time for him to take the throne. Fifteen years passed between his anointing and his coronation; and all that time his knowledge of what it meant to care for sheep deepened. Later, when he wrote a psalm celebrating God, it was natural for him to picture God as a shepherd over his life. Just as David had protected and cared for his sheep, so God had protected and cared for him.

David celebrated the God who was his shepherd.

JEHOVAH-JIREH: THE LORD SHALL PROVIDE

The first time the name appears in the Bible is in Genesis 22, the story of Abraham's obedience to God to offer his son, Isaac, as a sacrifice on Mount Moriah. The pain associated with Abraham sacrificing his own son is not the only problem in this story. God has told Abraham that from Isaac, and through his descendants, would flow all the blessings God had promised to Abraham (Genesis 12:1-3). It appeared that God had promised to bless Isaac and now was ordering his death.

We don't get the insight we need into what Abraham was thinking —why he was willing to obey God in this matter—until we get to the book of Hebrews in the New Testament (Hebrews 11:17-19). There we learn that Abraham concluded that, if God was going to bless Isaac and also put him to death, there would have to be a resurrection of Isaac from the dead. That was apparently okay with Abraham, so he went obediently to the mountain to sacrifice his son. We get a glimpse of Abraham's faith in this regard when he left the servants and started up the mountain with Isaac, telling the servants that he and Isaac would be returning to the servants (Genesis 22:5). Just as Abraham was about to kill Isaac with his knife, God intervened and provided a ram for Abraham to sacrifice. So Abraham named that place *Jehovah-Jireh*, or Jehovah Shall Provide.

Abraham celebrated the God who provides.

JEHOVAH-RAPHA: THE LORD WHO HEALS

In Exodus 15, we find the children of Israel in the wilderness. No longer did they have the food and water that was supplied for them in Egypt. In the wilderness they were thirsty, and sources of water were few and far between. Coming upon a water supply at an oasis called Marah, they rushed to get the water only to discover it was brackish— completely unfit for man or beast. If you've ever taken a mouthful of what used to be called "sulfur water" along the Florida coast or in some places in the Midwest, you know the taste.

The Israelites cried out to God in bitterness, asking why He had led them into such an inhospitable place. God told Moses to take a nearby branch and throw it into the pool of water and the water would be made sweet to the taste. Moses obeyed the Lord, the waters were changed, and the people's needs were met.

In His concluding remarks to Moses, God told him that their experience with the bitter water had been a test; that if they would walk in the Lord's commandments, He would keep them from experiencing any of the diseases He put upon the Egyptians—"For I am the Lord who heals you" (verse 26). So, in that place, Moses celebrated the Lord who heals.

JEHOVAH-NISSI: THE LORD MY BANNER

Farther along in the wilderness (Exodus 17), the children of Israel run into the warlike Amalekites, the descendants of Esau. This is not good for the Israelites who haven't picked up a sword in 430 years. And now the Amalekites don't want a couple million Israelites trespassing through their territory.

Moses sends Joshua out to fight with Amalek and takes Aaron and Hur to the top of a mountain with him to pray during the battle. When Moses lifts his hands up to the Lord in prayer, Israel prevails. When he takes his hands down to rest, Amalek prevails. So Aaron and Hur hold Moses' arms up so his hands remain lifted to the Lord in prayer until the battle is over and Israel defeats Amalek. To celebrate the victory the Lord had given, Moses builds an altar and names it The Lord Is My Banner, or *Jehovah-Nissi*.

Banner is not like a large banner or flag we might hang on the wall of a church or school today. The root of the Hebrew word reflects the meaning "to be high, raised, or conspicuous," and refers to a standard or rod raised as a rallying point for troops. Therefore, the Lord was to be Israel's rallying point in all things, the One around whom they would gather in times of need.

In that place, Moses celebrated the Lord around whom we gather for victory.

JEHOVAH-M'KADDESH: THE LORD WHO SANCTIFIES

One of my seminary professors used to refer to the book of Leviticus as the "pots and pans" book of the Bible because it has to do with all the worship ceremonies Israel was to carry out—lots of detail and "how-to" material. But all those instructions reflect the central theme of the book: the holiness of the Lord. Worship and sacrifice were to be carried out in such a way that the holiness of God and His people is reflected.

In chapter 20 we find this pivotal statement about all the regulations and stipulations that are found in Leviticus: "Consecrate yourselves therefore, and be holy, for I am the Lord your God. And you shall keep My statutes, and perform them: I am the Lord who sanctifies you" (verses 7-8). In the last phrase, we find yet another of the names of God in the Old Testament, *Jehovah-M'Kaddesh*, The Lord Who Sanctifies— Who Makes Holy.

The Lord is to be celebrated as the One who cleanses us and makes us holy.

JEHOVAH-SHALOM: THE LORD WHO IS PEACE

The next name comes from one of my favorite stories in Scripture, the story of Gideon in Judges 6–8. The judges ruled over Israel at a time when everyone was doing what seemed right in their own eyes. Time after time, Israel would turn away from the Lord, be judged by their enemies, be delivered by a judge God raised up, profess their allegiance to the Lord, and then repeat the cycle again.

Israel was being terrorized by the Midianites, and God raised up a farmer named Gideon to deliver the nation from Midian's attacks. Gideon was hiding at his threshing floor when the angel of the Lord approached him—he was dumbfounded that God wanted him to be the deliverer of Israel from the scourge of Midian. So Gideon accepts God's call and defeats the huge Midianite army with just a handful of soldiers. But at the beginning, Gideon was really uptight about being called to this new role—and who can blame him?

It wasn't until Gideon built an altar to worship *Jehovah-Shalom*, The Lord Who Is Peace (See Judges 6:24.), that he finally settled into his new role. He did that because the Lord said to him, "Peace be with you; do not fear, you shall not die" (verse 23).

Gideon celebrated the Lord who gives us every kind of peace.

JEHOVAH-TSIDKENU: THE LORD WHO IS RIGHTEOUS

The next name by which God is celebrated in the Old Testament is found in Jeremiah 23:5-6. Jeremiah prophesied at a time of great pain and sorrow in Jerusalem—Babylon was ransacking the nation and city as God's instrument of judgment on Judah's sins. When Jeremiah was called by God, he was told that no one would listen to his message of repentance and judgment but that he was not to lose heart over such rejection (Jeremiah 1:1-8).

God came to Jeremiah in the midst of his ministry and revealed Himself to the prophet in a new way:

"Behold, the days are coming," says the Lord,
"That I will raise to David a Branch of righteousness;
A King shall reign and prosper,
And execute judgment and righteousness in the earth.
In His days Judah will be saved,
And Israel will dwell safely;
Now this is His name by which He will be called:
THE LORD OUR RIGHTEOUSNESS."

In the midst of sin and destruction, God showed Jeremiah that a ruler was coming who would establish righteousness in the land, whose name would be *Jehovah-Tsidkenu*, or The Lord Who Is Righteous.

I have to believe Jeremiah built an altar and celebrated the Lord who is righteous.

JEHOVAH-SHAMMAH: THE LORD WHO IS THERE

The last of God's names appears in Ezekiel 48, the very last verse. Ezekiel's prophecy was similar to Jeremiah's, except he prophesied from Babylon where he had been taken in 597 B.C. He was given visions of the glory of God gradually departing from Jerusalem and Judah, and he prophesied about the coming destruction of Jerusalem in 586 B.C. But he was also shown a vision of a New Jerusalem that God would build, a magnificent city that dwarfed the original—"and the name of the city from that day shall be: THE LORD IS THERE" (verse 35).

To keep Ezekiel from despairing over the future of Jerusalem, God showed him a new name that meant God would once again reign in Jerusalem: *Jehovah-Shammah*, or The Lord Who Is There.

In Babylon, Ezekiel celebrated the Lord who would again be there among His people.

In closing, look how the names of God coincide with Psalm 23:

"The Lord is my shepherd"—*Jehovah-Rohi*
"I shall not want"—*Jehovah-Jireh*
"He makes me to lie down"—*Jehovah-Shalom*
"He restores my soul"—*Jehovah-Rapha*
"He leads me in the paths of righteousness"—*Jehovah-Tsidkenu*
"For You are with me"—*Jehovah-Shammah*
"In the presence of my enemies"—*Jehovah-Nissi*
"You anoint my head with oil"—*Jehovah-M'Kaddesh*

Psalm 23 is a shepherd's celebration of the Shepherd of his soul. I pray that through this series you have come to know better the God whom you worship and that your worship will become a daily celebration of who He is and what He has done in your life.

PERSONAL QUESTIONS

1. Read Psalm 23:1-6 written below.

   The Lord is my shepherd;
   I shall not want.
   He makes me to lie down in green pastures;
   He leads me beside the still waters.
   He restores my soul;
   He leads me in the paths of righteousness
   For His name's sake.

   Yea, though I walk through the valley of the shadow of death,
   I will fear no evil;
   For You are with me;
   Your rod and Your staff, they comfort me.

   You prepare a table before me in the presence of my enemies;
   You anoint my head with oil;
   My cup runs over.
   Surely goodness and mercy shall follow me
   All the days of my life;
   And I will dwell in the house of the Lord
   Forever.

   Highlight the lines that describe each of the eight names of God. Write the Hebrew names and their meaning next to each corresponding description.

2. What are the similarities between David being a shepherd and God being a Shepherd?

3. Read Genesis 12:1-3.

   a. What were the Lord's promises of provision to Abraham?

   b. How has the Lord protected and provided for you recently?

4. Read Leviticus 20:7-8. What does it mean to be sanctified?

GROUP QUESTIONS

1. How were the names of God ascribed to Him in the Bible?

2. List the eight names of God, as mentioned in this lesson, and what they reveal about His character.

  •

  •

  •

  •

  •

  •

  •

  •

3. Read Exodus 15:26 as a group.

   a. What did God say He would do for Moses and the Israelites if they obeyed His commandments?

b. Have you ever experienced the Lord's healing? What were the circumstances?

4. Read Exodus 17:14-16 together.

a. Can you think of any way the Lord has been your banner? If so, share with the group.

b. Have you had victory over something that seemed destined for defeat?

5. Turn to the section titled, "Jehovah-Shammah: The Lord Who Is There."

a. How did Ezekiel know the Lord would be present among His people in Babylon?

b. How can you experience the Lord who is there? Discuss.

c. Which of God's attributes have you praised Him for in worship?

6. As a group, share what you have learned from this lesson.

   a. What have these eight names of God revealed to you about who He is?

   b. Which name speaks to you the most? How so?

   c. Does Psalm 23 have a new meaning to you? Explain.

DID YOU KNOW?

Naming in the Bible carries much significance. Some names reflect their very essence, as when God set about naming things in creation: light, darkness, heaven, earth, seas, and more. Adam was allowed to name the animals in Eden (Genesis 2:19-20). He also gave the name "woman" (*ishah*) to his image-bearing counterpart because she was taken out of man (*ish*) (Genesis 2:23). He gave his wife the personal name "Eve" (*chawwa*) because she was the mother of all living (*cha*) (Genesis 3:20). Her son was named "Cain" (*qayin*) because she acquired (*qaniti*) him from the Lord (Genesis 4:1), and gave Seth (*shet*) his name because God appointed him (*shat*) (Genesis 4:25). God changed Abram's name (*avram*, "exalted father") to Abraham (*avraham*, "father of many") when He promised him many descendants (Genesis 17:5).

ADDITIONAL RESOURCES
by Dr. David Jeremiah

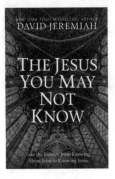

THE JESUS YOU MAY NOT KNOW

In *The Jesus You May Not Know,* Dr. Jeremiah answers probing questions about Jesus including: Is He From History or From Eternity? Is He the Teacher of Truth or the Truth to be Taught? Is He Praying for Us or Are We Praying to Him? Jesus is the mystery of the ages and the marvel of history. But He is also personable and knowable. Through this book, you will learn more about Him—the One who longs for your fellowship.

GOD LOVES YOU—HE ALWAYS HAS, HE ALWAYS WILL

God's love is not conditional. In *God Loves You,* Dr. David Jeremiah teaches us that the very nature of God is love—that God cannot be anything other than love. Understanding this is necessary in understanding God Himself. With this book, come to grasp the depth and breadth of God's love and let it transform your life today.

Each of these resources was created from a teaching series by Dr. David Jeremiah. Contact Turning Point for more information about correlating materials.

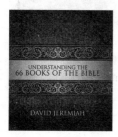

UNDERSTANDING THE 66 BOOKS OF THE BIBLE

Understanding the 66 Books of the Bible is a resource to orient you to each of God's special books whether you're a new reader or a veteran student, whether you want to visit the Gospel of John or take a journey into Nahum or Jude. In this volume by Dr. Jeremiah, you'll find a simple digest for each of the 66 books—Genesis to Revelation. After all, God's Word is a big book. It will be the fastest journey through the Bible you will ever experience!

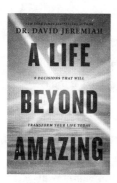

A LIFE BEYOND AMAZING

Each of us has just one life to live. Our life should count. It should matter. It should have purpose, and, frankly, it should be amazing. In *A Life Beyond Amazing*, Dr. David Jeremiah studies the fruit of the Spirit and discusses nine decisions that will transform your life. If you feel you haven't been living up to your full potential, discover how to live your life full of purpose for Christ.

For pricing information and ordering, contact us at

P.O. Box 3838
San Diego, CA 92163
(800) 947-1993
www.DavidJeremiah.org

STAY CONNECTED
to Dr. David Jeremiah

Take advantage of three great ways to let Dr. David Jeremiah
give you spiritual direction every day!

Turning Points Magazine and Devotional

Receive Dr. David Jeremiah's magazine,
Turning Points, each month:

- Thematic study focus
- 52 pages of life-changing reading
- Relevant articles
- Special features
- Daily devotional readings
- Bible study resource offers
- Live event schedule
- Radio & television information

Request *Turning Points* magazine today!
(800) 947-1993 | DavidJeremiah.org/Magazine

Daily Turning Point E-Devotional

Start your day off right! Find words of
inspiration and spiritual motivation waiting for
you on your computer every morning! Receive
a daily e-devotion communication from David
Jeremiah that will strengthen your walk with
God and encourage you to live the authentic
Christian life.

Sign up for your free e-devotional today!
www.DavidJeremiah.org/Devo

Turning Point Mobile App

Access Dr. David Jeremiah's video teachings,
audio sermons, and more... whenever and
wherever you are!

Download your free app today!
www.DavidJeremiah.org/App